D0198364

JavaScript
Pocket Reference

SECOND EDITION

JavaScript
Pocket Reference

David Flanagan

O'REILLY®

Beijing · Cambridge · Farnham · Köln · Paris · Sebastopol · Taipei · Tokyo

JavaScript Pocket Reference, Second Edition
by David Flanagan

Published by O'Reilly Media, Inc., 1005 Gravenstein Highway North,
Sebastopol, CA 95472.

O'Reilly Media, Inc. books may be purchased for educational,
business, or sales promotional use. Online editions are also available
for most titles (*safari.oreilly.com*). For more information contact our
corporate/institutional sales department: (800) 998-9938 or
corporate@oreilly.com.

Editor:	Paula Ferguson
Production Editor:	Philip Dangler
Cover Designer:	Edie Freedman
Interior Designer:	David Futato

Printing History:

October 1998:	First Edition
November 2002:	Second Edition

0-596-00411-7
[C]

Contents

JavaScript
Pocket Reference

The JavaScript Language

JavaScript is a lightweight, object-based scripting language that can be embedded in HTML pages. This book starts with coverage of the core JavaScript language, followed by material on client-side JavaScript, as used in web browsers. The final portion of this book is a quick-reference for the core and client-side JavaScript APIs.

Syntax

JavaScript syntax is modeled on Java syntax, Java syntax, in turn, is modeled on C and C++ syntax. Therefore, C, C++, and Java programmers should find that JavaScript syntax is comfortably familiar.

Case sensitivity

JavaScript is a case-sensitive language. All keywords are in lowercase. All variables, function names, and other identifiers must be typed with a consistent capitalization.

Whitespace

JavaScript ignores whitespace between tokens. You may use spaces, tabs, and newlines to format and indent your code in a readable fashion.

Semicolons

JavaScript statements are terminated by semicolons. When a statement is followed by a newline, however, the terminating semicolon may be omitted. Note that this places a restriction on where you may legally break lines in your JavaScript programs: you may not break a statement across two lines if the first line can be a complete legal statement on its own.

Comments

JavaScript supports both C and C++ comments. Any amount of text, on one or more lines, between /* and */ is a comment, and is ignored by JavaScript. Also, any text between // and the end of the current line is a comment, and is ignored. Examples:

```
// This is a single-line, C++-style comment.
/*
 * This is a multi-line, C-style comment.
 * Here is the second line.
 */
/* Another comment. */ // This too.
```

Identifiers

Variable, function, and label names are JavaScript *identifiers*. Identifiers are composed of any number of letters and digits, and _ and $ characters. The first character of an identifier must not be a digit, however. The following are legal identifiers:

```
i
my_variable_name
v13
$str
```

Keywords

The following keywords are part of the JavaScript language, and have special meaning to the JavaScript interpreter. Therefore, they may not be used as identifiers:

```
break     do        if          switch  typeof
case      else      in          this    var
catch     false     instanceof  throw   void
continue  finally   new         true    while
default   for       null        try     with
delete    function  return
```

JavaScript also reserves the following words for possible future extensions. You may not use any of these words as identifiers either:

```
abstract  enum        int        short
boolean   export      interface  static
byte      extends     long       super
char      final       native     synchronized
class     float       package    throws
const     goto        private    transient
debugger  implements  protected  volatile
double    import      public
```

In addition, you should avoid creating variables that have the same name as global properties and methods: see the Global, Object, and Window reference pages. Within functions, do not use the identifier arguments as an argument name or local variable name.

Variables

Variables are declared and initialized with the var statement:

```
var i = 1+2+3;
var x = 3, message = 'hello world';
```

Variable declarations in top-level JavaScript code may be omitted, but they are required to declare local variables within the body of a function.

JavaScript variables are *untyped*: they can contain values of any data type.

Global variables in JavaScript are implemented as properties of a special Global object. Local variables within functions are implemented as properties of the Argument object for

---

that function. Global variables are visible throughout a Java-
Script program. Variables declared within a function are only
visible within that function. Unlike C, C++, and Java, Java-
Script does not have block-level scope: variables declared
within the curly braces of a compound statement are not
restricted to that block and are visible outside of it.

Data Types

JavaScript supports three primitive data types: numbers,
booleans, and strings; and two compound data types: objects
and arrays. In addition, it defines specialized types of objects
that represent functions, regular expressions, and dates.

Numbers

Numbers in JavaScript are represented in 64-bit floating-
point format. JavaScript makes no distinction between integers and floating-point numbers. Numeric literals appear in
JavaScript programs using the usual syntax: a sequence of
digits, with an optional decimal point and an optional expo-
nent. For example:

```
1
3.14
0001
6.02e23
```

Integers may also appear in hexadecimal notation. A hexadecimal literal begins with 0x:

```
0xFF // The number 255 in hexadecimal
```

When a numeric operation overflows, it returns a special
value that represents positive or negative infinity. When an
operation underflows, it returns zero. When an operation
such as taking the square root of a negative number yields an
error or meaningless result, it returns the special value NaN,
which represents a value that is not-a-number. Use the global function isNaN( ) to test for this value.

The Number object defines useful numeric constants. The Math object defines various mathematical functions such as `Math.sin()`, `Math.pow()`, and `Math.random()`.

Booleans

The boolean type has two possible values, represented by the JavaScript keywords true and false. These values represent truth or falsehood, on or off, yes or no, or anything else that can be represented with one bit of information.

Strings

A JavaScript string is a sequence of arbitrary letters, digits, and other characters from the 16-bit Unicode character set.

String literals appear in JavaScript programs between single or double quotes. One style of quotes may be nested within the other:

```
'testing'
"3.14"
'name="myform"'
"Wouldn't you prefer O'Reilly's book?"
```

When the backslash character (\) appears within a string literal, it changes, or escapes, the meaning of the character that follows it. The following table lists these special escape sequences:

Escape	Represents
\b	Backspace
\f	Form feed
\n	Newline
\r	Carriage return
\t	Tab
\'	Apostrophe or single quote that does not terminate the string
\"	Double-quote that does not terminate the string
\\	Single backslash character

Escape	Represents
\x*dd*	Character with Latin-1 encoding specified by two hexadecimal digits *dd*
\u*dddd*	Character with Unicode encoding specified by four hexadecimal digits *dddd*

The String class defines many methods that you can use to operate on strings. It also defines the length property, which specifies the number of characters in a string.

The addition (+) operator concatenates strings. The equality (==) operator compares two strings to see if they contain exactly the same sequences of characters. (This is compare by-value, not compare-by-reference, as C, C++, or Java programmers might expect.) The inequality operator (!=) does the reverse. The relational operators(<, <=, >, and >=) compare strings using alphabetical order.

JavaScript strings are *immutable*, which means that there is no way to change the contents of a string. Methods that operate on strings typically return a modified copy of the string.

Objects

An *object* is a compound data type that contains any number of properties. Each property has a name and a value. The . operator is used to access a named property of an object. For example, you can read and write property values of an object o as follows:

```
o.x = 1;
o.y = 2;
o.total = o.x + o.y;
```

Object properties are not defined in advance as they are in C, C++, or Java; any object can be assigned any property. JavaScript objects are associative arrays: they associate arbitrary data values with arbitrary names. Because of this fact, object properties can also be accessed using array notation:

```
o["x"] = 1;
o["y"] = 2;
```

Objects are created with the new operator. You can create a new object with no properties as follows:

```
var o = new Object();
```

Typically, however, you use predefined constructors to create objects that are members of a class of objects and have suitable properties and methods automatically defined. For example, you can create a Date object that represents the current time with:

```
var now = new Date();
```

You can also define your own object classes and corresponding constructors; doing this is documented later in this section.

In JavaScript 1.2 and later, you can use object literal syntax to include objects literally in a program. An object literal is a comma-separated list of name:value pairs, contained within curly braces. For example:

```
var o = {x:1, y:2, total:3};
```

See Object (and Date) in the reference section.

Arrays

An array is a type of object that contains numbered values rather than named values. The [ ] operator is used to access the numbered values of an array:

```
a[0] = 1;
a[1] = a[0] + a[0];
```

The first element of a JavaScript array is element 0. Every array has a length property that specifies the number of elements in the array. The last element of an array is element length-1. Array elements can hold any type of value, including objects and other arrays, and the elements of an array need not all contain values of the same type.

You create an array with the `Array()` constructor:

```
var a = new Array();       // Empty array
var b = new Array(10);     // 10 elements
var c = new Array(1,2,3);  // Elements 1,2,3
```

As of JavaScript 1.2, you can use array literal syntax to include arrays directly in a program. An array literal is a comma-separated list of values enclosed within square brackets. For example:

```
var a = [1,2,3];
var b = [1, true, [1,2], {x:1, y:2}, "Hello"];
```

See Array in the reference section for a number of useful array manipulation methods.

Functions and methods

A function is a piece of JavaScript code that is defined once and can be executed multiple times by a program. A function definition looks like this:

```
function sum(x, y) {
  return x + y;
}
```

Functions are invoked using the () operator and passing a list of argument values:

```
var total = sum(1,2);  // Total is now 3
```

In JavaScript 1.1, you can create functions using the `Function()` constructor:

```
var sum = new Function("x", "y", "return x+y;");
```

In JavaScript 1.2 and later, you can define functions using function literal syntax, which makes the `Function()` constructor obsolete:

```
var sum = function(x,y) { return x+y; }
```

When a function is assigned to a property of an object, it is called a *method* of that object. Within the body of a method, the keyword this refers to the object for which the function is a property.

Within the body of a function, the arguments[ ] array contains the complete set of arguments passed to the function. See Function and Arguments in the reference section.

null and undefined

There are two JavaScript values that are not of any of the types described above. The JavaScript keyword null is a special value that indicates "no value". If a variable contains null, you know that it does not contain a valid value of any other type. The other special value in JavaScript is the undefined value. This is the value of uninitialized variables and the value returned when you query object properties that do not exist. In JavaScript 1.5, there is a pre-defined global variable named undefined that holds this special undefined value. null and undefined serve similar purposes and the == operator considers them equal; if you need to distinguish between them, use the === operator.

Expressions and Operators

JavaScript expressions are formed by combining values (which may be literals, variables, object properties, array elements, or function invocations) using JavaScript operators. Parentheses can be used in an expression to group subexpressions and alter the default order of evaluation of the expression. Some examples:

```
1+2
total/n
sum(o.x, a[3])++
```

JavaScript defines a complete set of operators, most of which should be familiar to C, C++, and Java programmers. They are listed in the table below, and a brief explanation of the non-standard operators follows. The P column specifies operator precedence and the A column specifies operator associativity: L means left-to-right associativity, and R means right-to-left associativity.

P	A	Operator	Operation performed
15	L	.	Access an object property
	L	[ ]	Access an array element
	L	( )	Invoke a function
	R	new	Create new object
14	R	++	Pre-or-post increment (unary)
	R	--	Pre-or-post decrement (unary)
	R	-	Unary minus (negation)
	R	+	Unary plus (no-op)
	R	~	Bitwise complement (unary)
	R	!	Logical complement (unary)
	R	delete	Undefine a property (unary) (JS 1.2)
	R	typeof	Return data type (unary) (JS 1.1)
	R	void	Return undefined value (unary) (JS 1.1)
13	L	*, /, %	Multiplication, division, remainder
12	L	+, -	Add, subtract
	L	+	Concatenate strings
11	L	<<	Integer shift left
	L	>>	Shift right, sign-extension
	L	>>>	Shift right, zero extension
10	L	<, <=	Less than, less than or equal
	L	>, >=	Greater than, greater than or equal
	L	instanceof	Check object type (JS 1.5)
	L	in	Check whether property exists (JS 1.5)
9	L	==	Test for equality
	L	!=	Test for inequality
	L	===	Test for identity (JS 1.3)
	L	!==	Test for non-identity (JS 1.3)

P	A	Operator	Operation performed
8	L	&	Integer bitwise AND
7	L	^	Integer bitwise XOR
6	L	|	Integer bitwise OR
5	L	&&	Logical AND
4	L	||	Logical OR
3	R	?:	Conditional operator (3 operands)
2	R	=	Assignment
	R	*=, +=, -=, etc.	Assignment with operation
1	L	,	Multiple evaluation

JavaScript operators that are not familiar from C, C++, and Java are the following:

=== *and* !==

The JavaScript equality operator, ==, defines equality loosely and allows type conversions. For example, it considers the number 3 and the string "3" to be equal, it considers false to be equal to 0, and it considers null and undefined to be equal. The identity operator, ===, written with three equals signs, is stricter: it only evaluates to true if its operands are identical: i.e. if they have the same type and are equal. Similarly, the JavaScript non-identity operator !== is stricter than the non-equality != operator.

String operators

In JavaScript, the + operator concatenates string arguments in addition to adding numeric arguments. The == and === operators compare strings by value by testing to see whether they contain exactly the same characters. The relational operators <, <=, >, and >= compare strings based on alphabetical order.

typeof
> Return the type of the operand as a string. Evaluates to "number", "string", "boolean", "object", "function", or "undefined". Evaluates to "object" if the operand is null.

instanceof
> Evaluates to true if the object on the left was created with the constructor function (such as Date or RegExp) on the right.

in
> Evaluates to true if the object on the right has (or inherits) a property with the name on the left.

delete
> Deletes an object property. Note that this is not the same as simply setting the property to null. Evaluates to false if the property could not be deleted, or true otherwise.

void
> Ignores the operand and evaluates to undefined.

Statements

A JavaScript program is a sequence of JavaScript statements. Most JavaScript statements have the same syntax as the corresponding C, C++, and Java statements.

Expression statements

Every JavaScript expression can stand alone as a statement. Assignments, method calls, increments, and decrements are expression statements. For example:

```
s = "hello world";
x = Math.sqrt(4);
x++;
```

Compound statements

When a sequence of JavaScript statements is enclosed within curly braces, it counts as a single compound statement. For

---

example, the body of a while loop consists of a single statement. If you want the loop to execute more than one statement, use a compound statement. This is a common technique with if, for, and other statements described later.

Empty statements

The empty statement is simply a semicolon by itself. It does nothing, and is occasionally useful for coding empty loop bodies.

Labeled statements

As of JavaScript 1.2, any statement can be labeled with a name. Labeled loops can then be used with the labeled versions of the break and continue statements:

```
label : statement
```

Alphabetical statement reference

The following paragraphs document all JavaScript statements, in alphabetical order.

break

> The break statement terminates execution of the innermost enclosing loop, or, in JavaScript 1.2 and later, the named loop:
>
> ```
> break ;
> break label ;
> ```

case

> case is not a true statement. Instead it is a keyword used to label statements within a JavaScript 1.2 or later switch statement:
>
> ```
> case constant-expression :
>     statements
>     [ break ; ]
> ```
>
> Because of the nature of the switch statement, a group of statements labeled by case should usually end with a break statement.

continue

> The continue statement restarts the innermost enclosing loop, or, in JavaScript 1.2 and later, restarts the named loop:
>
> ```
> continue ;
> continue label ;
> ```

default

> Like case, default is not a true statement, but instead a label that may appear within a JavaScript 1.2 or later switch statement:
>
> ```
> default:
>     statements
>     [ break ; ]
> ```

do/while

> The do/while loop repeatedly executes a statement while an expression is true. It is like the while loop, except that the loop condition appears (and is tested) at the bottom of the loop. This means that the body of the loop is executed at least once:
>
> ```
> do
>     statement
> while ( expression ) ;
> ```
>
> This statement was introduced in JavaScript 1.2. In Netscape 4, the continue statement does not work correctly within do/while loops.

for

> The for statement is an easy-to-use loop that combines the initialization and increment expressions with the loop condition expression:
>
> ```
> for (initialize ; test ; update )
>     statement
> ```
>
> The for loop repeatedly executes statement as long as the test expression is true. It evaluates the initialize expression once before starting the loop and evaluates the update expression at the end of each iteration.

for/in

The for/in statement loops through the properties of a specified object:

```
for (variable in object)
    statement
```

The for/in loop executes a statement once for each property of an object. Each time through the loop, it assigns the name of the current property to the specified variable. Some properties of pre-defined JavaScript objects are not enumerated by the for/in loop. User-defined properties are always enumerated.

function

The function statement defines a function in a JavaScript program:

```
function funcname ( args ) {
    statements
}
```

This statement defines a function named *funcname*, with a body that consists of the specified statement, and arguments as specified by *args*. *args* is a comma-separated list of zero or more argument names. These arguments can be used in the body of the function to refer to the parameter values passed to the function.

if/else

The if statement executes a statement if an expression is true:

```
if ( expression )
    statement
```

When an else clause is added, the statement executes a different statement if the expression is false:

```
if ( expression )
    statement
else
    statement2
```

Any else clause may be combined with a nested if/else statement to produce an else if statement:

```
if ( expression )
    statement
else if ( expression2 )
    statement2
else
    statement3
```

return

> The return statement causes the currently executing
> function to stop executing and return to its caller. If fol-
> lowed by an expression, the value of that expression is
> used as the function return value:
>
> ```
> return ;
> return expression ;
> ```

switch

> The switch statement is a multi-way branch. It evaluates
> an expression and then jumps to a statement that is
> labeled with a case clause that matches the value of the
> expression. If no matching case label is found, the switch
> statement jumps to the statement, if any, labeled with
> default:
>
> ```
> switch ( expression ) {
>     case constant-expression: statements
>     [ case constant-expression: statements ]
>     [ . . . ]
>     default: statements
> }
> ```
>
> Each set of statements within a switch statement is usu-
> ally terminated with a break or return so that execution
> does not fall through from one case to the next one.

throw

> The throw statement signals an error, or throws an excep-
> tion. It causes program control to jump immediately to
> the nearest enclosing exception handler (see the try/
> catch/finally statement). The throw statement is defined
> by ECMAv3 and implemented in JavaScript 1.5. Its syn-
> tax is:
>
> ```
> throw expression ;
> ```

The *expression* may evaluate to any type. (See Error in the reference section.)

try/catch/finally

The try/catch/finally statement is JavaScript's exception handling mechanism. It is defined by ECMAv3 and implemented in JavaScript 1.5. Its syntax is:

```
try {
    statements
}
catch ( argument ) {
    statements
}
finally {
    statements
}
```

The try clause of this statement defines a block of code for which exceptions and errors are to be handled. If a program error occurs, or an exception is thrown within the try block, control jumps to the exception-handling statements in the catch clause. This clause includes a single argument or local variable; the value that was thrown by the exception is assigned to this local variable so that it can be referred to by the statements of the catch clause. The finally clause contains statements that are executed after the try or catch clauses, whether or not an exception is thrown. The catch and finally clauses are optional, but you cannot omit both of them.

var

The var statement declares and optionally initializes one or more variables. Variable declaration is optional in top-level code, but is required to declare local variables within function bodies:

```
var name [ = value ] [ , name2 [ = value2 ]  . . .  ]
;
```

while

> The while statement is a basic loop. It repeatedly executes a statement while an expression is true:

```
while ( expression )
    statement ;
```

with

> The with statement adds an object to the scope chain, so that a statement is interpreted in the context of the object:

```
with ( object )
    statement ;
```

The with statement has some complex and non-intuitive side effects; its use is strongly discouraged.

Object-Oriented JavaScript

JavaScript objects are associative arrays that associate values with named properties. JavaScript provides a simple inheritance mechanism, and it is possible to define new classes of objects for use in your own programs. To define a new class, start by writing a constructor function. A constructor is like any other function, except it is invoked with the new operator and it uses the this keyword to refer to and initialize the newly created object. For example, here is a constructor to create objects of a new class named Point.

```
function Point(x,y) { // Constructor for Point
  this.x = x;  // Initialize X coordinate
  this.y = y;  // Initialize Y coordinate
}
```

Every JavaScript function used as a constructor has a property named prototype. This property refers to a special prototype object for the class of objects created by the constructor. Any properties you define on this prototype object are inherited by all objects created with the constructor function. The prototype object is commonly used to make methods available to all instances of a class. Defining a method named toString

---

allows instances of your class to be converted to strings. For example:

```
// Define function literals and assign them
// to properties of the prototype object.
Point.prototype.distanceTo = function(that) {
  var dx = this.x - that.x;
  var dy = this.y - that.y;
  return Math.sqrt(dx*dx + dy*dy);
}
Point.prototype.toString = function () {
  return '(' + this.x + ',' + this.y + ')';
}
```

If you want to define static (or class) methods or properties, you can assign them directly to the constructor function, rather than to the prototype object. For example:

```
// Define a commonly used Point constant
Point.ORIGIN = new Point(0,0);
```

The preceding code fragments define a simple Point class that we can use with code like this:

```
// Call constructor to create a new Point object
var p = new Point(3,4);
// Invoke a method of the object, using a static
// property as the argument.
var d = p.distanceTo(Point.ORIGIN);
// Adding the object to a string implicitly
// invokes toString().
var msg = "Distance to " + p + " is " + d;
```

Regular Expressions

JavaScript supports regular expressions for pattern matching with the same syntax as the Perl programming language. JavaScript 1.2 supports Perl 4 regular expressions, and JavaScript 1.5 adds supports for some of the additional features of Perl 5 regular expressions. A regular expression is specified literally in a JavaScript program as a sequence of characters within slash (/) characters, optionally followed by one or more of the modifier characters g (global search), i (case-insensitive search), and m (multi-line mode; a JavaScript 1.5

feature). In addition to this literal syntax, RegExp objects can be created with the RegExp() constructor, which accepts the pattern and modifier characters as string arguments, without the slash characters.

A full explanation of regular expression syntax is beyond the scope of this book, but the tables in the following subsections offer brief syntax summaries.

Literal characters

Letters, numbers, and most other characters are literals in a regular expression: they simply match themselves. As we'll see in the sections that follow, however, there are a number of punctuation characters and escape sequences (beginning with \) that have special meanings. The simplest of these escape sequences provide alternative ways of representing literal characters:

Character	Meaning
\n, \r, \t	Match literal newline, carriage return, tab
\\, \/, *, \+, \?, etc.	Match a punctuation character literally, ignoring or escaping its special meaning
\x*nn*	The character with hexadecimal encoding *nn*.
\u*xxxx*	The Unicode character with hexadecimal encoding *xxxx*.

Character classes

Regular expression syntax uses square brackets to represent character sets or classes in a pattern. In addition, escape sequences define certain commonly-used character classes, as shown in the following table.

Character	Meaning
[...]	Match any one character between brackets
[^ ...]	Match any one character not between brackets
.	Match any character other than newline

Character	Meaning
\w, \W	Match any word/non-word character
\s, \S	Match any whitespace/non-whitespace
\d, \D	Match any digit/non-digit

Repetition

The following table shows regular expression syntax that controls the number of times that a match may be repeated.

Character	Meaning
?	Optional term; Match zero or one time
+	Match previous term one or more times
*	Match previous term zero or more times
{n}	Match previous term exactly *n* times
{n,}	Match previous term *n* or more times
{n,m}	Match at least *n* but no more than *m* times

In JavaScript 1.5, any of the repetition characters may be followed by a question mark to make them non-greedy, which means they match as few repetitions as possible while still allowing the complete pattern to match.

Grouping and alternation

Regular expressions use parentheses to group subexpressions, just as mathematical expressions do. Parentheses are useful, for example, to allow a repetition character to be applied to an entire subexpression. They are also useful with the | character, which is used to separate alternatives. Parenthesized groups have a special behavior: when a pattern match is found, the text that matches each group is saved and can be referred to by group number. The following table summarizes this syntax.

Character	Meaning
a | b	Match either *a* or *b*
(sub)	Group subexpression *sub* into a single term, and remember the text that it matched
(?:sub)	Group subexpression *sub* but do not number the group or remember the text it matches (JS 1.5)
\n	Match exactly the same characters that were matched by group number *n*
$n	In replacement strings, substitute the text that matched the *n*th subexpression

Anchoring match position

An *anchor* in a regular expression matches a position in a string (such as the beginning or the end of the string) without matching any of the characters of a string. It can be used to restrict (or anchor) a match to a specific position within a string.

Character	Meaning
^, $	Require match at beginning/end of a string, or in multiline mode, beginning/end of a line
\b, \B	Require match at a word boundary/non-boundary
(?=p)	Look-ahead assertion: require that the following characters match the pattern *p*, but do not include them in the match. (JS 1.5)
(?!p)	Negative look-ahead assertion: require that the following characters do not match the pattern *p*. (JS 1.5)

Versions of JavaScript

Netscape has defined a number of versions of JavaScript. Microsoft has released more-or-less compatible versions under the name "JScript," and the ECMA standards body has released three versions of a JavaScript standard named "ECMAScript". The following paragraphs describe these various versions, and explain how they relate to each other. Each entry in the reference section contains availability information that documents the version of JavaScript in which a feature was introduced.

JavaScript 1.0

The original version of the language. It was buggy and is now essentially obsolete. Implemented by Netscape 2.

JavaScript 1.1

Introduced a true Array object; most serious bugs resolved. Implemented by Netscape 3.

JavaScript 1.2

Introduced the switch statement, regular expressions, and a number of other features. Almost compliant with ECMA v1, but has some incompatibilities. Implemented by Netscape 4.

JavaScript 1.3

Fixed incompatibilities of JavaScript 1.2. Compliant with ECMA v1. Implemented by Netscape 4.5.

JavaScript 1.4

Only implemented in Netscape server products.

JavaScript 1.5

Introduced exception handling. Compliant with ECMA v3. Implemented by Mozilla and Netscape 6.

JScript 1.0

Roughly equivalent to JavaScript 1.0. Implemented by early releases of IE 3.

JScript 2.0

Roughly equivalent to JavaScript 1.1. Implemented by later releases of IE 3.

JScript 3.0

Roughly equivalent to JavaScript 1.3. Compliant with ECMA v1. Implemented by IE 4.

JScript 4.0

Not implemented by any web browser.

JScript 5.0

Supported exception handling; partial ECMA v3 compliance. Implemented by IE 5.

JScript 5.5

Roughly equivalent to JavaScript 1.5. Fully compliant with ECMA v3. Implemented by IE 5.5 and IE 6.

ECMA v1

The first standard version of the language. Standardized the basic features of JavaScript 1.1 and added a few new features. Did not standardize the switch statement or regular expression support. Conformant implementations are JavaScript 1.3 and JScript 3.0.

ECMA v2

A maintenance release of the standard that included clarifications but defined no new features.

ECMA v3

Standardized the switch statement, regular expressions, and exception handling. Conformant implementations are JavaScript 1.5 and JScript 5.5.

Client-side JavaScript

Client-side JavaScript is the name given to JavaScript code that is embedded within an HTML file and executed by a web browser. In addition to the core objects described in the previous section, client-side JavaScript code has access to a number of other objects that represent the web browser, the document displayed in the browser, and the contents of that document. Client-side JavaScript programs are usually event-based, which means that JavaScript *event handlers* are executed in response to user interactions with the browser and the document. The client-side JavaScript scripting framework is powerful enough to open substantial security holes in web browsers. For this reason, web browsers typically restrict the actions of client-side scripts. This section starts by

---

explaining how JavaScript code is embedded in HTML files, then goes on to introduce the client-side JavaScript objects, JavaScript events and event handling, and JavaScript security restrictions.

JavaScript in HTML

JavaScript code may be embedded in HTML files in the form of scripts, event handlers and URLs, as detailed below.

The <script> tag

Most JavaScript code appears in HTML files between a <script> tag and a </script> tag. For example:

```
<script>
document.write("The time is: " + new Date());
</script>
```

In JavaScript 1.1 and later you can use the src attribute of the <script> tag to specify the URL of an external script to be loaded and executed. Files of JavaScript code typically have a *.js* extension. Note that the </script> tag is still required when this attribute is used:

```
<script src="library.js"></script>
```

HTML allows scripts to be written in languages other than JavaScript, and some browsers, such as Internet Explorer, support languages such as VBScript. You can use the language attribute to specify what language a script is written in. This attribute defaults to "JavaScript" in all browsers, so you do not usually have to set it. You can also use attribute values such as "JavaScript1.3" and "JavaScript1.5" to specify the version of JavaScript your code uses. Browsers that do not support the specified version of the language simply ignore the script.

HTML 4 does not actually recognize the language attribute of the <script> tag. Instead, the official way to specify the language a script is written in is with the type attribute. For Java-Script, set this attribute to the MIME type "text/javascript":

```
<script src="functions.js"
        language="JavaScript1.5"
        type="text/javascript"></script>
```

Event handlers

JavaScript code may also appear as the value of an event handler attribute of an HTML tag. Event handler attribute names always begin with "on". The code specified by one of these attributes is executed when the named event occurs. For example, the following HTML creates a button, and the onclick attribute specifies an event handler that displays an alert (a dialog box) when the user clicks the button:

```
<input type="button" value="Press Me"
       onclick="alert('Hello World!');">
```

A list of other available event handler attributes is included later in this section.

JavaScript URLs

JavaScript code may appear in a URL that uses the special javascript: pseudo-protocol. The content of such a URL is determined by evaluating the JavaScript code and converting the resulting value to a string. If you want to use a JavaScript URL to execute JavaScript code without returning any document content that would overwrite the current document, use the void operator:

```
<form action="javascript:void validate()">
```

The Window Object

The Window object represents a web browser window. In client-side JavaScript, the Window object is the global object that defines all top-level properties and methods. The properties and methods of the Window object are therefore global properties and global functions and you can refer to them

---

by their property names without any object prefix. One of the properties of the Window object is named `window` and refers back to the Window object itself:

```
window              // The global Window object
window.document     // The document property of the window
document            // Or omit the object prefix
```

See the Window object in the reference section for a full list of its properties and methods. The following sections summarize the most important of these properties and methods and demonstrate key client-side programming techniques using the Window object. Note that the most important property of the Window object is `document`, which refers to the Document object that describes the document displayed by the browser window. The Document object is described in a section of its own following these window-related subsections.

Simple dialog boxes

Three methods allow you to display simple dialog boxes to the user. `alert()` lets you display a message to the user, `confirm()` lets you ask the user a yes-or-no question, and `prompt()` lets you ask the user to enter a single line of text. For example:

```
alert("Welcome to my home page!");
if (confirm("Do you want to play?")) {
    var n = prompt("Enter your name");
}
```

The status line

Most web browsers include a status line at the bottom of the window that is used to display the destination of links and other information. You can specify text to appear in the status line with the `status` property. The text you set on this property appears in the status area until you or the browser overwrites it with some new value. You can also set `defaultStatus` to specify text to appear by default when the browser is not displaying any other information in the status line. Here is an HTML hyperlink that uses JavaScript in an event handler to set the status text to something other than the URL of the link:

```
<a href="help.html"
    onmouseover="window.status='Help'; return true;">
Help</a>
```

Timers

Client-side JavaScript uses event handlers to specify code to be run when a specific event occurs. You can also use timers to specify code to be run when a specific number of milliseconds has elapsed. To run a string of JavaScript code after a specified amount of time, call the setTimeout() method, passing the string of code and the number of milliseconds. If you want to run a string of code repeatedly, use setInterval() to specify the code to run and the number of milliseconds between invocations. Both functions return a value that you can pass to clearTimeout() or clearInterval(), respectively, to cancel the pending execution of code. For example:

```
var count = 0;
// Update status line every second
var timer = setInterval("status=++count",1000);
// But stop updating after 5 seconds;
setTimeout("clearInterval(timer)", 5000);
```

System information

The navigator and screen properties of the Window object refer to the Navigator and Screen objects, which themselves define properties that contain system information, such as the name and version of the web browser, the operating system it is running on, and the resolution of the user's screen. See Navigator and Screen in the reference section for details. The Navigator object is commonly used when writing code specific to a particular web browser or web browser version:

```
if (navigator.appName == "Netscape" &&
    parseInt(navigator.appVersion) == 4) {
  // Code for Netscape 4 goes here.
}
```

Browser navigation

The `location` property of the Window object refers to the contents of the browser's location bar (the field that you type URLs into). Reading the value of this property gives you the URL that is currently being displayed. More importantly, setting the `location` property to a new URL tells the browser to load and display the document referred to by that URL:

```
// In old browsers, load a different page
if (parseInt(navigator.appVersion) <= 4)
    location = "staticpage.html";
```

Note that any script or event handler that sets the `location` property of its own window (we'll discuss multiple windows and multiple frames later in this section) is overwritten when the new document is loaded and will not continue running!

Although the `location` property can be queried and set as if it were a string, it actually refers to a Location object. The Location object has properties that allow you to query and set individual portions of the currently displayed URL:

```
// Get the substring of the URL following ?
var query = location.search.substring(1);
// Scroll to a named portion of the document
location.hash = "#top";
```

In addition, the `reload()` method makes the browser reload the currently displayed URL.

The `history` property of the Window object refers to the History object for the browser window. This object defines methods that allow you to move the browser backward and forward through its browsing history, just as the user can with the browser's **Back** and **Forward** buttons:

```
history.back();    // Go back once
history.forward(); // Go forward
history.go(-3);    // Go back three times
```

Window control

The Window object defines methods to move, resize, and scroll windows, and methods to give keyboard focus to and take focus away from windows. For example:

```
// Automatically scroll 10 pixels a second
setInterval("scrollBy(0,1)", 100);
```

See moveTo(), moveBy(), resizeTo(), resizeBy(), scrollTo() scrollBy(), focus() and blur() in the Window object entry of the reference section for more information.

More important than these methods that manipulate an existing window are the open() method that creates a new browser window and the close() method that closes a script-created window. The open() method takes three arguments. The first is the URL to be displayed in the new window. The second is an optional name for the window. If a window by that name already exists, it is reused and no new window is created. The third argument is an optional string that specifies the size of the new window and the features, or chrome, that it should display. For example:

```
// Open a new window
w = open("new.html", "newwin", // URL and name
        "width=400,height=300," + // size
        "location,menubar," +      // chrome
        "resizable,scrollbars,status,toolbar");
// And close that new window
w.close();
```

Note that most browsers only allow scripts to close windows that they have opened themselves. Also, because of the recent proliferation of nuisance pop-up advertisements on the Web, some browsers do not allow scripts to open new windows at all.

Multiple windows and frames

As discussed previously, the open() method of the Window object allows you to create new browser windows that are represented by new Window objects. The window that a script is running in is the global object for that script, and you can use all the properties and methods of that Window object as if they were globally defined. When a script running in one window needs to control or interact with a different window, however, you must explicitly specify the Window object:

```
// Create a new window and manipulate it
var w = open("newdoc.html");
w.alert("Hello new window");
w.setInterval("scrollBy(0,1)",50);
```

HTML allows a single window to have multiple frames. Many web designers choose to avoid frames, but they are still in fairly common use. JavaScript treats each frame as a separate Window object, and scripts in different frames run independently of each other. The frames property of the Window object is an array of Window objects, representing the subframes of a window:

```
// Scripts in framesets refer to frames like this:
frames[0].location = "frame1.html";
frames[1].location = "frame2.html";
// With deeply nested frames, you can use:
frames[1].frames[2].location = "frame2.3.html";
// Code in a frame refers to the top-level window:
top.status = "Hello from the frame";
```

The parent property of a Window object refers to the containing frame or window. The top property refers to the top-level browser window that is at the root of the frame hierarchy. (If the Window object represents a top-level window rather than a frame, the parent and top properties simply refer to the Window object itself.)

Each browser window and frame has a separate JavaScript execution context, and in each context, the Window object is the global object. This means that any variables declared or functions defined by scripts in the window or frame become properties of the corresponding Window object. This allows a script in one window or frame to use variables and functions defined in another window or frame. It is common, for example, to define functions in the <head> of a top-level window, and then have scripts and event handlers in nested frames call those functions using the top property:

```
// Code in a frame calls code in the top-level window.
top.stop_scrolling();
```

The Document Object

Every Window object has a document property that refers to a Document object. The Document object is arguably more important than the Window object itself: while the Window represents the browser window, the Document object represents the HTML document that is displayed in that window. The Document object has various properties that refer to other objects which allow access to and modification of document content. The way that document content is accessed and modified is called the document object model, or DOM, and there are several DOMs in existence:

Legacy DOM
> The original legacy document object model evolved along with early versions of the JavaScript language. It is well supported by all browsers, but allows access only to certain key portions of documents, such as forms, form elements, and images.

W3C DOM
> This document object model allows access and modification of all document content and is standardized by the World Wide Web Consortium (W3C). It is at least partially supported by Netscape 6 and later, Internet Explorer 5 and later, and other modern browsers. The W3C DOM is not closely compatible with the IE 4 DOM, but it does standardize many of the legacy features of the original DOM. This book covers the core features of the standard, and presents a simplified subset of the DOM relevant for JavaScript programmers working with HTML documents. You can find complete coverage in *JavaScript: The Definitive Guide*.

IE 4 DOM

Microsoft's Internet Explorer Version 4 extended the legacy DOM with powerful new features for accessing and modifying all content of a document. These features were never standardized, but some of them are supported in non-Microsoft browsers.

The following sections explain each of these DOMs in more detail and describe how you can use them to access and modify document content.

The Legacy DOM

The original client-side JavaScript DOM defines provides access to document content through properties of the Document object. Several read-only properties, such as `title`, `URL`, and `lastModified` provide information about the document as a whole. See the reference section for further details on these and all Document properties and methods. Other properties are arrays that refer to specific types of document content:

`forms[ ]`

An array of Form objects representing the forms in a document.

`images[ ]`

An array of Image objects representing the images that appear in a document.

`applets[ ]`

An array of objects that represent the Java applets embedded in a document. JavaScript can actually be used to script Java and control these applets, but doing so is beyond the scope of this pocket reference.

`links[ ]`

An array of Link objects representing the hyperlinks in the document.

```
anchors[ ]
```
An array of Anchor objects representing the anchors (named positions created with the name attribute of the HTML <a> tag) in the document.

These arrays contain objects in the order they appear in the document. So the first form in a document is document.forms[0], and the third image is document.images[2]. Another way to refer to document forms, images, and applets is to give them names with the HTML name attribute:

```
<form name="address">...</form>
```

When an form, image, or applet is given a name in this way, you can use that name to look it up in the array, or to look it up directly as a property of the document itself:

```
document.forms["address"]  // A named form
document.address           // The same thing
```

The Form object is particularly interesting. It has an elements[ ] array that contains objects representing the elements of the form, in the order they appear in the form. See Input, Select, and Textarea in the reference section for details on these form elements.

The elements[ ] array of a Form works much like the forms[ ] array of a Document: it holds form elements in the order they appear in the form, but it also allows them to be referred to by name. Consider this HTML excerpt:

```
<form name='address'><input name='street'></form>
```

You can refer to the input element of the form in several ways:

```
document.forms[0].elements[0]
document.address.elements['street']
document.address.street
```

The legacy DOM does not provide any way to refer to document content other than forms, form elements, images, applets, links, and anchors. There is no array that provides a list of all <h1> tags, for example, nor is there any way for a script to obtain the actual text of a document. This is a short-coming that is addressed by the W3C and IE 4 DOMs, as we'll see later. Although it is limited, the legacy DOM does allow scripts to dynamically alter some document content, as we'll see in the following subsections.

Dynamically generated documents

In addition to the properties already described, the Document object defines several important methods for dynamically generating document content. Use the write() method to output text into the document at the location of the <script> that contains the method calls. For example:

```
document.write("<p>Today is: " + new Date());
document.write("<p>Document updated: " +
  document.lastModified);
```

Note that text output in this way may contain arbitrary HTML tags; the browser parses and displays any such text after executing the script that output it.

The write() method can be used from a <script> tag only while a document is still loading. If you try to use it within an event handler that is triggered after the document has loaded, it erases the document and the event handler it contains. It is legal, however, to use an event handler in one window or frame to trigger a document.write() call into another window. When you do this, however, you must write the complete contents of the new document, and remember to call the document.close() method when you are done:

```
var clock = open("", "", "width=400,height=30");
var d = clock.document; // Save typing below
setInterval("d.write(new Date());d.close();",
            1000);
```

Dynamic forms

As we've seen, the elements[] array of a Form object contains objects that represent the input elements of the form. Many of these objects have properties that you can use to query or set the value displayed in the form element. This provides another way to dynamically change document content. For example, the following code sets the value property of a Text object to display the current local time.

```
<form><input size=10></form>  // An HTML form
<script>  /* Display a clock in the form */
// The Text element we're working with.
var e = document.forms[0].elements[0];
// Code to display the time in that element
var s="e.value=(new Date()).toLocaleTimeString();"
setInterval(s, 1000); // Run it every second
</script>
```

Form validation

The <form> tag supports an onsubmit event handler, which is triggered when the user tries to submit a form. You can use this event handler to perform *validation*: checking that all required fields have been filled in, for example. If the onsubmit handler returns false, the form is not submitted. For example:

```
<form name="address" onsubmit="checkAddress()">
<!-- form elements go here -->
</form>
<script>
// A simple form validation function
function checkAddress() {
  var f = document.address; // The form to check
  // Loop through all elements
  for(var i = 0; i < f.elements.length; i++) {
    // Ignore all but text input elements
    if (f.elements[i].type != "text") continue;
    // Get the user's entry
    var text = f.elements[i].value;
    // If it is not filled in, alert the user
    if (text == null || text.length == 0) {
      alert("Please fill in all form fields.");
      return false;
    }
  }
}
</script>
```

Image rollovers

The legacy DOM allows you to accomplish one common special effect: dynamically replacing one image on the page with another. This is often done for image rollovers, in which an image changes when the mouse moves over it. The images[] array of the Document object contains Image objects that represent the document's images. Each Image object has a src property that specifies the URL of the image to be displayed. To change the image that is displayed, simply set this property to a new URL:

```
document.images[0].src = "newbanner.gif";
```

To use this technique for an image rollover, you must use it in conjunction with the onmouseover and onmouseout event handlers that are triggered when the mouse moves on to and off of the image. Here is some basic HTML code with Java-Script event handlers to accomplish a rollover:

```
<img name="button" src="b1.gif"
    onmouseover="document.button.src='b2.gif';"
    onmouseout="document.button.src='b1.gif';">
```

When an image is going to be dynamically displayed, it is helpful to preload it into the browser cache so that there is no network delay before it appears. You can do this with a dynamically created off-screen Image object:

```
var i = new Image(); // Create Image object
i.src="b2.gif";      // Load, but don't display image
```

Working with cookies

The cookie property of the Document object is a peculiar one that allows you to set and query the cookies associated with your document. To associate a transient cookie with the document, simply set the cookie property to a string of the form:

name=value

This creates a cookie with the specified *name* and *value* for this document. If you want to create a cookie that is stored even when the user quits the browser, add an expiration date using a string of the form:

```
name=value; expires=date
```

The expiration *date* should be in the form returned by Date.toGMTString(). If you want the cookie to be accessible to other documents from your web site, you can specify a path prefix:

```
name=value; expires=date; path=prefix
```

A single document may have more than one cookie associated with it. To query a document's cookies, simply read the value of the cookie property. This string contains *name=value* strings separated from each other by a semicolon and a space. When reading cookies, you'll never see a "path=" or "expires=" clause; you'll just get the cookie name and value. Here's a function that retrieves the value of a single named cookie from the cookie property. It assumes that cookie values never contain semicolons.

```
function getCookie(name) {
  // Split cookies into an array
  var cookies = document.cookie.split('; ');
  for(var i = 0; i < cookies.length; i++) {
    var c = cookies[i];            // One cookie
    var pos = c.indexOf('=');      // Find = sign
    var n = c.substring(0,pos);    // Get name
    if (n == name)                 // If it matches
      return c.substring(pos+1);   // Return value
  }
  return null;  // Can't find the named cookie
}
```

The W3C DOM

The W3C DOM standardizes most of the features of the legacy DOM, but also adds important new ones. In addition to supporting forms[ ], images[ ], and other array properties of the Document object, it defines methods that allow scripts to access and manipulate any document element, not just special-purpose elements like forms and images.

Finding elements by ID

When creating a document that contains special elements that will be manipulated by a script, you can identify each special element by giving it an id attribute with a unique value. Then, you can use the getElementById() method of the Document object to look up those elements by their ID:

```
<h1 id="title">Title</h1>
<script>
var t = document.getElementById("title");
</script>
```

Finding elements by tag name

Another way to access document elements is to look them up by tag name. The getElementsByTagName() method of the Document object returns an array of all elements of that type. Each document element also supports the same method, so you can also obtain an array of specific types of tags that are all descendents of an element:

```
// Get an array of all <ul> tags
var lists = document.getElementsByTagName("ul");
// Find the 3rd <li> tag in the second <ul>
var item = lists[1].getElementsByTagName("li")[2];
```

Traversing a document tree

The W3C DOM represents every document as a tree. The nodes of this tree represent the HTML tags, the strings of text, and the HTML comments that comprise the document. Each node of the tree is represented by a JavaScript object, and each has properties that allow you to traverse the tree, as illustrated by the following code fragment:

```
// Look up a node in the document
var n = document.getElementById("mynode");
var p = n.parentNode;  // The containing tag
var c0 = n.firstChild;    // First child of n
```

```
var c1 = c0.nextSibling;  // 2nd child of n
var c2 = n.childNodes[2]; // 3rd child of n
var last = n.lastChild;   // last child of n
```

See Node in the reference section for further details.

The Document object itself is a kind of node, and supports these same properties. The documentElement property of the Document object refers to the single <html> tag element at the root of all HTML documents, and the body property refers to the <body> tag.

Node types

Every node in a document tree has a nodeType property that specifies what type of node it is. Different types of nodes are represented by different subclasses of the Node object. The following nodeType values are relevant to JavaScript programmers working with HTML documents (other values exist for XML documents):

nodeType	Represents
1	Element: an HTML tag
2	Text: text in a document
8	Comment: an HTML comment
9	Document: the HTML document

Use the nodeName property of an Element node to determine the name of the HTML tag it represents. Use the nodeValue property of Text and Comment nodes to obtain the document text or comment text represented by the node. See Element, Text, Comment, and Document in the reference section for details on each of these node types. Also see Node for information on the common properties and methods they all share.

HTML attributes

As we've seen above, HTML tags in a document tree are represented by Element objects. In HTML documents, each Element object has properties that correspond directly to the attributes of the HTML tag. For example, you can query or set the value of the caption attribute of a `<table>` tag by setting the caption property of the corresponding Element object. See Element in the reference section for details.

Manipulating document elements

One easy way to manipulate HTML documents with the W3C DOM is simply to set the properties that correspond to HTML attributes. As we saw in the legacy DOM, this allows you to change images by setting the src property of the document element that represents an `<img>` tag, for example. It also allows you to set colors, sizes, and alignments of document elements. One particularly fruitful way to manipulate document elements is through the style property which controls CSS styles. We'll cover this important topic in more detail later.

Changing document text

You can change the textual content of a document simply by setting the nodeValue property of a Text node:

```
// Find the first <h1> tag in the document
var h1 = document.getElementsByTagName("h1")[0];
// Set new text of its first child
h1.firstChild.nodeValue = "New heading";
```

In addition to manipulating the nodeValue property, the Text object also allows you to modify the data property, or to use methods to append, insert, delete or replace text.

Note that the problem with the previous code is that it assumes that the content of the `<h1>` tag is plain text. The code would fail for a document with the following heading because the text of the heading is a grandchild of the `<h1>` tag rather than a direct child:

```
<h1><i>Original Heading</i></h1>
```

One way around this problem is to set the `innerHTML` property of the heading node. This property is part of the IE 4 DOM, not the W3C DOM, but it is supported by most modern browsers because it is so useful. We'll see it again when we consider the IE 4 DOM. Another way around the problem is to replace the heading node with a newly created `<h1>` tag and text node containing the desired text, as shown in the next section.

Changing document structure

In addition to changing document text and the attributes of document elements, the W3C DOM allows you to alter the tree structure of the document itself. This is done with Node methods that allow you to insert, append, remove, and replace children of a node and with Document methods that allow you to create new Element and Text nodes. The following code illustrates:

```
// Find a <ol> element by name:
var list = document.getElementById("mylist");
// Create a new <li> element
var item = document.createElement("li");
// Append it to the list
list.appendChild(item);
// Create a Text node
var text = document.createTextNode("new item");
// Append it to the new <li> node
item.appendChild(text);
// Remove the new item from the list
list.removeChild(item);
// Place the new item at the start of the list
list.insertBefore(item,list.firstChild);
```

As a further example, here is a JavaScript function that uses the W3C DOM to embolden an arbitrary document node by reparenting it within a newly created `<b>` tag:

```
function embolden(node) {  // Embolden node n
  var b = document.createElement("b");
  var p = n.parentNode; // Get parent of n
  p.replaceChild(b, n); // Replace n with <b>
  b.appendChild(n);      // Insert n into <b> tag
}
```

IE 4 DOM

The IE 4 DOM was introduced in Version 4 of Microsoft's
Internet Explorer browser. It is a powerful but non-standard
DOM with capabilities similar to those of the W3C DOM. IE
5 and later include support for most basic W3C DOM features, but this documentation on the IE 4 DOM is included
because IE 4 is still commonly used. The following subsections document the IE 4 DOM in terms of its differences
from the W3C DOM, so you should be familiar with the
W3C DOM first.

Accessing document elements

The IE 4 DOM does not support the getElementById()
method. Instead, it allows you to look up arbitrary document elements by id attribute within the all[] array of the
document object:

```
var list = document.all["mylist"];
list = document.all.mylist;  // this also works
```

Instead of supporting the getElementsByTagName() method,
the IE 4 DOM takes the unusual step of defining a tags()
method on the all[] array, which exists on document elements as well as the Document object itself. Here's how to
find all <li> tags within the first <ul> tag:

```
var lists = document.all.tags("UL");
var items = lists[0].all.tags("LI");
```

Note that you must specify the desired HTML tag name in
uppercase with the all.tags() method.

Traversing the document tree

You can traverse an IE 4 document tree in much the same way that you can traverse a W3C document tree. The difference is in the names of the relevant properties: instead of `childNodes[]`, IE 4 uses `children[]`, and instead of `parentNode`, IE 4 uses `parentElement`. IE 4 does not have any analogs to `firstChild`, `nextSibling`, and related W3C properties. One important difference between the IE 4 and W3C DOMs is that the IE 4 document tree only includes HTML tags: comments are ignored and document text is not part of the tree itself. Instead, the text contained by any element is available through the `innerHTML` and `innerText` properties of the element object. (We'll see more about `innerHTML` in the next section.)

Modifying document content and structure

The nodes of an IE 4 document tree are Element objects that are similar to the Element node of the W3C DOM. Like the Element nodes of a W3C document tree, these objects have properties that correspond to the attributes of the HTML tags, and you can query and set the properties as desired. To change the textual content of a document element, set its `innerText` property to the desired text. This deletes any existing tags or text within the element and replaces it with the specified text.

The IE 4 DOM does not have any methods for explicitly creating, inserting, removing, or replacing nodes of the document tree. However, it does support the very important `innerHTML` property, which allows you to replace the content of any document element with an arbitrary string of HTML. Doing this requires an invocation of the HTML parser, making it less efficient than manipulating the nodes directly. On the other hand, it is tremendously convenient, so much so that Mozilla, Netscape 6 and later, and other modern browsers have implemented `innerHTML` despite the fact that it is non-standard.

The IE 4 DOM also includes the related `outerHTML` property, which replaces the element and its content, and the `insertAdjacentHTML()` and `insertAdjacentText()` methods. These are not as commonly used, nor as commonly implemented outside of IE as `innerHTML`; you can read about them in the reference section under Element.

DOM compatibility

If you want to write a script that uses the W3C DOM when it is available, and otherwise uses the IE 4 DOM if it is available, you can use a capability-testing approach that first checks for the existence of a method or property to determine whether the browser has the capability you desire. For example:

```
if (document.getElementById) {
    // If the W3C method exists, use it
}
else if (document.all) {
    // If the all[] array exists, use it
}
else {
    // Otherwise use the legacy DOM
}
```

DHTML: Scripting CSS Styles

DHTML, or Dynamic HTML, is the result of combining HTML, CSS, and JavaScript: it uses scripts to dynamically modify the style—which may include the position and visibility—of document elements. In the W3C and the IE 4 DOMs, every document element has a `style` property that corresponds to the HTML `style` attribute that specifies inline styles. Instead of referring to a simple string, however, the `style` property refers to a Style object that has properties corresponding to each of the CSS attributes of the style.

For example, if an element e has a `style` attribute that specifies the CSS `color` attribute, you can query the value of that attribute as `e.style.color`. When a CSS attribute name contains hyphens, the corresponding JavaScript property name removes the hyphens and uses mixed-case capitalization. Thus, to set the `background-color` CSS attribute of an element e, you set `e.style.backgroundColor`. There is one special case: the CSS `float` attribute is a reserved word in JavaScript, so the corresponding JavaScript property is `cssFloat`.

The CSS standard defines many properties that you can use to fine-tune the visual appearance of your documents. The Style entry in the reference section includes a table that lists them all. The positioning and visibility properties are particularly relevant for dynamic scripting. If the `position` property is set to `absolute`, you can use the `top` and `left` properties to specify the absolute position (in pixels, percentages, or other units) of the document element. Similarly, the `width` and `height` properties specify the size of the element. The `visibility` property can initially be set to `hidden` to make a document element invisible, and then dynamically set to `visible` to make the element appear when appropriate.

Note that the values of all Style properties are always strings, even for properties like `left` and `width` which represent numbers. When setting these length and dimension properties, be sure to convert your numbers to strings and to add the appropriate units specification (usually the string `px` for pixels.) The following table summarizes these positioning and visibility properties:

Property	Description/Values
position	How the element is positioned. `absolute`, `relative`, `fixed`, or `static` (the default).
left, top	The X and Y coordinates of the left and top edges of the element.
width	The width of the element.
height	The height of the element.
zIndex	The stacking order. Values are integers; higher values are drawn on top of lower values.
display	How to display the element. Common values are `block`, `inline`, and `none` for elements that don't get laid out at all.

Property	Description/Values
visibility	Whether the element is visible or hidden. Space is still allocated for non-positioned hidden elements.
overflow	What to do when element content exceeds element size. Values: visible (content overflows); hidden (excess content hidden); scroll (display permanent scrollbar); auto (scrollbars only when needed).
clip	What portion of element content to display. Syntax: rect(*top right bottom left*).

The following code shows a simple DHTML animation. Each time it is called, the function nextFrame() moves an element 10 pixels to the right and uses setTimeout() to tell Java-Script to call it again in 50 milliseconds. After 20 invocations, the function uses the visibility property to hide the element and stops calling itself.

```
<h1 id='title'>DHTML Animation<h1>
<script>
// Look up the element to animate
var e = document.getElementById("title");
// Make it position-able.
e.style.position = "absolute";
var frame = 0;  // Initialize frame counter.
// This function moves the element one frame
// at a time, then hides it when done.
function nextFrame() {
  if (frame++ < 20) { // Only do 20 frames
    e.style.left = (10 * frame) + "px";
    // Call ourselves again in 50ms.
    setTimeout("nextFrame()", 50);
  }
  else e.style.visibility="hidden"; // Hide it.
}
nextFrame();  // Start animating now!
</script>
```

Events and Event Handling

We saw at the beginning of this section that one way to embed client-side JavaScript into HTML documents is to use event handler attributes of HTML tags. The following table lists the standard event handler attributes and the HTML tags to which they may be applied. The first column of the table gives the event handler attribute name: these names always begin with "on". The second column of the table lists the HTML tags to which these attributes can be applied, and explains, when necessary, what events trigger the handler code to be executed.

Handler	Supported by/Triggered when
onabort	`<img>`; image load aborted
onblur	`<body>` and form elements; window or element loses keyboard focus
onchange	Form elements; displayed value changes
onclick	All elements; mouse press and release; return `false` to cancel
ondblclick	All elements; mouse double-click
onerror	`<img>`; image loading fails
onfocus	`<body>` and form elements; window or element gets keyboard focus
onkeydown	`<body>` and form elements; key pressed; return `false` to cancel
onkeypress	`<body>` and form elements; key pressed and released; return `false` to cancel
onkeyup	`<body>` and form elements; key released
onload	`<body>`, `<frameset>`, `<img>`, `<iframe>`, `<object>`; document, image, or object completely loaded
onmousedown	All elements; mouse button pressed
onmousemove	All elements; mouse pointer moved
onmouseout	All elements; mouse moves off element
onmouseover	All elements; mouse moves over element; return `true` to prevent link URL display in status bar
onmouseup	All elements; mouse button released
onreset	`<form>`; form reset requested; return `false` to prevent reset
onresize	`<body>`, `<frameset>`; window size changes
onsubmit	`<form>`; form submission requested; return `false` to prevent submission
onunload	`<body>`, `<frameset>`; document unloaded

Note that when the browser triggers certain event handlers, such as `onclick`, `onmouseover` and `onsubmit`, it examines the return value of the handler (if there is one) to determine whether it should perform the default action associated with the event or not. Typically, if an event handler returns `false`, the default action (such as following a hyperlink or submitting a form) is not performed. The one exception is for the `onmouseover` handler: when the mouse moves over a hyperlink, the browser displays the link's URL in the status line unless the event handler returns `true`.

Event handlers as JavaScript functions

We've seen that the various document object models represent HTML tags as JavaScript objects, with the attributes of those tags as properties of the objects. The same is true of event handlers. If your HTML document includes a single `<form>` tag with an `onsubmit` event handler attribute, that event handler is available as:

```
document.forms[0].onsubmit
```

Although HTML event handler attributes are written as strings of JavaScript code, the value of the corresponding JavaScript properties are not strings of code, but actual Java-Script functions. You can create a new event handler simply by assigning a function to the appropriate property:

```
function validate() { // Form validation function
  // check validity here
  return valid;       // return true or false
}
// Now check user input before submitting it
document.forms[0].onsubmit = validate;
```

Advanced event handling

The previous sections describe the basic event-handling model for client-side JavaScript. Advanced event-handling features are also available, but unfortunately, there are three incompatible event models: the standard W3C DOM model, the Internet Explorer model (Microsoft has not adopted the W3C standard), and the Netscape 4 model. These event models are complex, so the following list simply summarizes the advanced features supported by these models. For details consult *JavaScript: The Definitive Guide*.

Event details

In the advanced event handling models, event details such as event type, mouse buttons and coordinates, modifier key state, and so on, are provided through the properties of an Event object. In the W3C and Netscape event models, this Event object is passed as an argument to the event handler. In the IE model, the Event object is not an argument but is instead stored in the event property of the Window on which the event occurs. Unfortunately, each of the three advanced event models use different property names to store event details, so cross-browser compatibility is difficult. See Event in the reference section for documentation of each of the three types of Event objects.

Event propagation

In the basic event model, event handlers are triggered only for the document element on which the event occurred. In the advanced models, events can propagate up and/or down the element hierarchy and be handled by one or more event handlers. In the Netscape and W3C models, events start at the document object and propagate down through the document tree to the element on which they occurred. If any of the containing elements have special capturing event handlers registered, these event handlers capture the event and get first crack at handling it. In the IE and W3C models, certain types of events (such as mouse clicks) bubble up the document tree after being handled at their source. Thus, you might register an onclick event handler on a <div> object in order to handle all mouse clicks that occur on elements within that <div>. Capturing, bubbling, and normal event handlers have the option of preventing the event from propagating any further, although the way this is done is different in each model.

Event handler registration
In the W3C event model, event handlers are not simply assigned to properties of document objects. Instead, each document object has an `addEventListener()` method that you call to register an event handler function for a named type of event. This allows advanced applications to register more than one handler for the same event type.

JavaScript Security Restrictions

For security reasons, client-side JavaScript implementations typically impose restrictions on the tasks that scripts can perform. The most obvious restrictions are omissions of dangerous capabilities: there is no way for client-side JavaScript to delete files on a user's local hard disk, for example. Other restrictions exist to prevent the disclosure of private information or to keep scripts from annoying users. There is no standard set of security restrictions, but the following are restrictions found in typical browser implementations. Don't attempt to write scripts that do these things: even if they work for your browser, they probably won't work in others.

Same origin policy
Scripts can only read properties of windows and documents that were loaded from the same web server. This is a substantial and pervasive restriction on cross-window scripting, and prevents scripts from reading information from other unrelated documents that the user is viewing. This restriction also prevents scripts from registering event handlers or spoofing events on unrelated documents.

File uploads
Scripts cannot set the `value` property of the FileUpload form element.

Sending email and posting news
> Scripts cannot submit forms to mailto: or news: URLs without user confirmation.

Closing windows
> A script can only close browser windows that it created itself, unless it gets user confirmation.

Snooping in the cache
> A script cannot load any about: URLs, such as about: cache.

Hidden windows and window decorations
> A script cannot create small or offscreen windows or windows without a titlebar.

Note that this list of security restrictions is not static. As the use of JavaScript has grown, advertisers and unsavory characters have started doing annoying things with it. As a result, newer browsers, such as Mozilla 1.0, allow user-configurable security restrictions that can prevent scripts from opening new windows (such as pop-up ads), or from moving or resizing existing windows.

JavaScript API Reference

The rest of this book contains a quick-reference for the core and client-side JavaScript APIs. It documents the complete core JavaScript API, covers the legacy (Level 0) DOM API, and presents a simplified view of the W3C Level 2 DOM API. Portions of that API not relevant to JavaScript programmers working with HTML documents have been omitted. The upper-right corner of the title block for each reference entry contains information that states whether a feature is part of the core or client-side API, and further indicates which version of JavaScript, which browsers, or which version of the DOM introduced the feature.

Because JavaScript is a loosely-typed language, there is not an official set of class names for the classes and objects of the JavaScript API, and they sometimes appear under different names in different references. (For brevity, this book actually uses a slightly different set of names than its big brother, *JavaScript: The Definitive Guide*.) The following table summarizes the reference entries that follow, and allows you to quickly scan for the class or object you are interested in.

Anchor	A named position in a document
Applet	A Java applet
Arguments	The arguments of a function
Array	Array creation and manipulation
Attr	An attribute of a document element
Boolean	A wrapper object for boolean values
Comment	An HTML comment
DOMException	Signals DOM errors
DOMImplementation	Creates documents, checks DOM features
Date	Manipulates dates and times
Document	An HTML document
DocumentFragment	Nodes to be manipulated together
Element	An HTML tag in a document
Error	Predefined exception types
Event	Event details
Form	An HTML input form
Function	A JavaScript function
Global	Global properties and functions
History	Browsing history
Image	An HTML image
Input	A form input element
Layer	An independent document layer
Link	An <a> or <area> link
Location	Current browser location
Math	Mathematical functions and constants
Navigator	Information about the browser
Node	A node in a document tree
Number	Support for numbers
Object	The superclass of all JavaScript objects
Option	A selectable option

RegExp	Regular expressions for pattern matching
Screen	Information about the display
Select	A graphical selection list
String	String manipulation
Style	Inline CSS properties of an element
Text	A run of text in a document
Textarea	Multiline text input
Window	Browser window or frame

Anchor

Client-side JavaScript 1.2

a named position in a document

Inherits From: Element

Synopsis

```
document.anchors[index]
document.anchors[name]
```

Description

An Anchor object represents an <a> tag with a name attribute, which serves to create a named position in a document.

Properties

name
    The value of the name attribute of the <a> tag.

See Also

Document.anchors[ ], Link, Location.hash

Applet

Client-side JavaScript 1.1

a Java applet

Synopsis

```
document.applets[i]
document.applets[appletName]
document.appletName
```

Properties & Methods

The properties and methods of an Applet object are the same as the public fields and methods of the Java applet it represents. JavaScript code can query and set the Java fields and invoke the Java methods of the applet.

Arguments

the arguments of a function

Synopsis

```
arguments[n]
arguments.length
```

Description

The Arguments object is defined only within a function body, and within every function body, the local variable arguments refers to the Arguments object for that function. The Arguments object is an array whose elements are the values that were passed as arguments to the function. Element 0 is the first argument, element 1 is the second argument, and so on. All values passed as arguments become array elements of the Arguments object, whether or not those arguments are given names in the function declaration.

Properties

callee
    A reference to the function that is currently executing. Useful for recursion in unnamed functions. JS 1.2; JScript 5.5; ECMA v1; only defined within a function body.

length
    The number of arguments passed to the function. JS 1.1; JScript 2; ECMA v1; only defined within a function body.

See Also

Function

Array

array creation and manipulation

Constructor

```
new Array()              // empty
new Array(n)             // n undefined elements
new Array(e0, e1,...)    // specified elements
```

Literal Syntax

In JavaScript 1.2, JScript 3.0, and ECMA v3, you can create and initialize an array by placing a comma-separated list of expressions within square brackets. The values of these expressions become the elements of the array. For example:

```
var a = [1, true, 'abc'];
var b = [a[0], a[0]*2, f(x)];
```

Properties

length
  A read/write integer specifying the number of elements in the array, or, when the array does not have contiguous elements, a number one larger than the index of the last element in the array. Changing the value of this property truncates or extends the array.

Methods

concat(value, ...)
  Returns a new array, which is formed by concatenating each of the specified arguments to this one. If any arguments to concat() are themselves arrays, their elements are concatenated, rather than the arrays themselves. JS 1.2; JScript 3.0; ECMA v3.

join(separator)
  Returns the string that results from converting each element of an array to a string and then concatenating the strings together, with the separator string between elements.

pop()
  Removes and returns the last element of the array, decrementing the array length. JS 1.2; JScript 5.5; ECMA v3.

---

push(*value,* ...)

> Appends the specified value or values to the end of the array, and returns the new length of the array. JS 1.2; JScript 5.5; ECMA v3.

reverse()

> Reverses the order of the elements of an array. Returns nothing.

shift()

> Removes and returns the first element of the array, shifting subsequent elements down one and decrementing the array length. JS 1.2; JScript 5.5; ECMA v3.

slice(*start, end*)

> Returns a new array that contains the elements of the array from the element numbered *start,* up to, but not including, the element numbered *end.* JS 1.2; JScript 3.0; ECMA v3.

sort(*orderfunc*)

> Sorts the elements of an array, and returns a reference to the array. Note that the array is sorted in place and no copy is made. The optional *orderfunc* argument may specify a function that defines the sorting order. The function should expect two arguments and should return a value that is less than 0 if the first argument is less than the second, 0 if they are equal, and a value greater than 0 if the first is greater than the second.

splice(*start, deleteCount, value,*...)

> Deletes the specified number of elements from the array starting at the specified index, then inserts any remaining arguments into the array at that location. Returns an array containing the deleted elements. JS 1.2; JScript 5.5; ECMA v3.

toLocaleString()

> Returns a localized string representation of the array. JS 1.5; JScript 5.5; ECMA v1.

toString()

> Returns a string representation of *array.*

unshift(*value,* ...)

> Inserts the argument or arguments as new elements at the beginning of an array, shifting existing array elements up to make room. Returns the new length of the array. JS 1.2; JScript 5.5; ECMA v3.

Attr

an attribute of a document element

Properties

name

> The name of the attribute. Read-only.

ownerElement

> The Element object that contains this attribute. Read-only. DOM Level 2.

specified

> true if the attribute was explicitly specified in the document source or set by a script. false otherwise. Read-only.

value

> The value of the attribute as a string. Read/write.

See Also

Document.createAttribute(),   Element.getAttributeNode(),
Element.setAttributeNode()

Boolean

a wrapper object for boolean values

Constructor

```
new Boolean(value)
Boolean(value)
```

Invoked as a function, without the new operator, Boolean() converts *value* to a boolean value (not a Boolean object) and returns it. All values convert to true except for 0, NaN, null, undefined, and the empty string, "". When invoked with the new operator, the Boolean() constructor performs the same conversion and wraps the result in a Boolean object.

Methods

toString()
    Returns "true" or "false", depending on the value of the Boolean object.

valueOf()
    Returns the primitive boolean value wrapped by the Boolean object.

Comment   DOM Level 1

an HTML comment   Inherits From: Node

Properties

Comment nodes have exactly the same properties as Text nodes.

Methods

Comment nodes support all of the methods of Text nodes except for splitText().

See Also

Text

DOMException   DOM Level 1

signals DOM errors

Properties

code
    An error code that provides some detail about what caused the exception. Some possible values (and their meanings) for this property are defined by the constants listed below.

Constants

The following constants define the code values that may be encountered by when working with HTML documents. Note that these constants are static properties of DOMException, not properties of individual exception objects.

DOMException.INDEX_SIZE_ERR = 1
> Out-of-bounds error for an array or string index.

DOMException.HIERARCHY_REQUEST_ERR = 3
> An attempt was made to place a node somewhere illegal in the document tree hierarchy.

DOMException.WRONG_DOCUMENT_ERR = 4
> An attempt was made to use a node with a document other than the document that created the node.

DOMException.INVALID_CHARACTER_ERR = 5
> An illegal character was used (in an element name, for example).

DOMException.NOT_FOUND_ERR = 8
> A node was not found where it was expected.

DOMException.NOT_SUPPORTED_ERR = 9
> A method or property is not supported in the current DOM implementation.

DOMException.INUSE_ATTRIBUTE_ERR = 10
> An attempt was made to associate an Attr with an Element when that Attr node was already associated with a different Element node.

DOMException.SYNTAX_ERR = 12
> A syntax error occurred, such as in a CSS property specification.

DOMImplementation   DOM Level 1

creates documents, checks DOM features

Synopsis

```
document.implementation
```

Methods

createHTMLDocument(*title*)

Creates and returns a new HTML Document object and populates it with <html>, <head>, <title>, and <body> elements. *title* is the text to appear in the <title> element. DOM Level 2.

hasFeature(*feature*, *version*)

Returns true if the implementation supports the specified version of the specified feature, or false otherwise. If no version number is specified, the method returns true if the implementation completely supports any version of the specified feature. Both *feature* and *version* are strings; for example, "core", "1.0" or "html", "2.0".

Date   Core JavaScript 1.0; JScript 1.0; ECMA v1

manipulates dates and times

Constructor

```
new Date();              // current time
new Date(milliseconds)   // from timestamp
new Date(datestring);    // parse string
new Date(year, month, day,
         hours, minutes, seconds, ms)
```

With no arguments, the Date() constructor creates a Date object set to the current date and time. When one numeric argument is passed, it is taken as the internal numeric representation of the date in milliseconds, as returned by the getTime() method. When one string argument is passed, it is taken as a string representation of a date. Otherwise, the constructor is passed between two and seven numeric arguments that specify the individual fields of the local date and time. All but the first two arguments—the year and month fields—are optional. See the static Date.UTC() method for an alternative that uses universal time instead of local time.

When called as a function without the new operator, Date() ignores any arguments passed to it and returns a string representation of the current date and time.

Methods

The Date object has no properties; instead, all access to date and time values is done through methods. Most methods come in two forms: one that operates using local time, and one that has "UTC" in its name and operates using universal (UTC or GMT) time. These pairs of methods are listed here. Note that the return values and optional arguments described below for most set( ) methods are not supported prior to ECMA standardization. See the various get( ) methods for the legal ranges for most of the various date fields.

get[UTC]Date( )

> Returns the day of the month, in local or universal time. Return values are between 1 and 31.

get[UTC]Day( )

> Returns the day of the week, in local or universal time. Return values are between 0 (Sunday) and 6 (Saturday).

get[UTC]FullYear( )

> Returns the year in full four-digit form, in local or universal time. JS 1.2; JScript 3.0; ECMA v1.

get[UTC]Hours( )

> Returns the hours field, in local or universal time. Return values are between 0 (midnight) and 23 (11 p.m.).

get[UTC]Milliseconds( )

> Returns the milliseconds field, in local or universal time. Return values are between 0 and 999. JS 1.2; JScript 3.0; ECMA v1.

get[UTC]Minutes( )

> Returns the minutes field, in local or universal time. Return values are between 0 and 59.

get[UTC]Month( )

> Returns the month field, in local or universal time. Return values are between 0 (January) and 11 (December).

get[UTC]Seconds( )

> Returns the seconds field, in local or universal time. Return values are between 0 and 59.

getTime( )

Returns the internal millisecond representation of the date; that is, returns the number of milliseconds between midnight (UTC) of January 1st, 1970 and the date and time represented by the Date object. Note that this value is independent of timezone.

getTimezoneOffset( )

Returns the difference, in minutes, between the local and UTC representations of this date. Note that the value returned depends on whether daylight savings time is or would be in effect at the specified date.

getYear( )

Returns the year field minus 1900. Deprecated in favor of getFullYear( ).

set[UTC]Date(*day_of_month*)

Sets the day of the month field, using local or universal time. Returns the millisecond representation of the adjusted date.

set[UTC]FullYear(*year, month, day*)

Sets the year (and optionally the month and day), using local or universal time. Returns the millisecond representation of the adjusted date. JS 1.2; JScript 3.0; ECMA v1

set[UTC]Hours(*hours, mins, secs, ms*)

Sets the hour (and optionally the minutes, seconds, and milliseconds fields), using local or universal time. Returns the millisecond representation of the adjusted date.

set[UTC]Milliseconds(*millis*)

Sets the milliseconds field of a date, using local or universal time. Returns the millisecond representation of the adjusted date. JS 1.2; JScript 3.0; ECMA v1.

set[UTC]Minutes(*minutes, seconds, millis*)

Sets the minutes field (and optionally the seconds and milliseconds fields) of a date, using local or universal time. Returns the millisecond representation of the adjusted date.

set[UTC]Month(*month, day*)

Sets the month field (and optionally the day of the month) of a date using local or universal time. Returns the millisecond representation of the adjusted date.

set[UTC]Seconds(*seconds, millis*)

Sets the seconds field (and optionally the milliseconds field) of a date, using local or universal time. Returns the millisecond representation of the adjusted date.

setTime(*milliseconds*)

Sets the internal millisecond date representation. Returns the *milliseconds* argument.

setYear(*year*)

Sets the 2-digit year field. Deprecated in favor of set[UTC]FullYear().

toDateString()

Returns a string that represents the date portion of the date, expressed in the local timezone. JS 1.5; JScript 5.5; ECMA v3.

toGMTString()

Converts a Date to a string, using the GMT timezone, and returns the string. Deprecated in favor of toUTCString().

toLocaleDateString()

Returns a string that represents the date portion of the date, expressed in the local time zone, using the local date formatting conventions. JS 1.5; JScript 5.5; ECMA v3.

toLocaleString()

Converts a Date to a string, using the local timezone and the local date formatting conventions.

toLocaleTimeString()

Returns a string that represents the time portion of the date, expressed in the local time zone, using the local time formatting conventions. JS 1.5; JScript 5.5; ECMA v3.

toString()

Returns a string representation of the date using the local timezone.

toTimeString()

Returns a string that represents the time portion of the date, expressed in the local timezone. JS 1.5; JScript 5.5; ECMA v3.

toUTCString()

Converts a Date to a string, using universal time, and returns the string. JS 1.2; JScript 3.0; ECMA v1.

valueOf()
> Returns the millisecond representation of the date, exactly as getTime() does. JS 1.1; ECMA v1.

Static Functions

In addition to the previously listed instance methods, the Date object defines two static methods. These methods are invoked through the Date() constructor itself, not through individual Date objects:

Date.parse(*date*)
> Parses a string representation of a date and time and returns the internal millisecond representation of that date.

Date.UTC(*yr, mon, day, hr, min, sec, ms*)
> Returns the millisecond representation of the specified UTC date and time.

Document
Client-side JavaScript 1.0; DOM Level 1

an HTML document
Inherits From: Node (in DOM Level 1)

Synopsis

```
window.document
document
```

Description

The Document object represents an HTML document and is one of the most important objects in client-side JavaScript. It was introduced in JavaScript 1.0, and a number of methods and properties were added in JavaScript 1.1. Netscape and Internet Explorer each add non-standard methods and properties to the Document object, and the W3C DOM standardizes additional properties and methods.

Common Properties

All implementations of the Document object support the following properties. This list is followed by separate lists of properties defined by the W3C DOM Document object and by the IE 4 and Netscape 4 Document objects.

alinkColor

A string that specifies the color of activated links. Deprecated.

anchors[ ]

An array of Anchor objects, one for each anchor that appears in the document. JS 1.2.

applets[ ]

An array of Applet objects, one for each applet that appears in the document. JS 1.1.

bgColor

A string that specifies the background color of the document. Deprecated.

cookie

A string-valued property with special behavior that allows the cookies associated with this document to be queried and set.

domain

A string that specifies the Internet domain the document is from. Used for security purposes. JS 1.1.

embeds[ ]

An array of objects that represent data embedded in the document with the <embed> tag. A synonym for plugins[ ]. Some plugins and ActiveX controls can be controlled with JavaScript code. The API depends on the specific control. JS 1.2 .

fgColor

A string that specifies the default text color for the document. Deprecated.

forms[ ]

An array of Form objects, one for each HTML form that appears in the document.

images[ ]

An array of Image objects, one for each image that is embedded in the document with the HTML <img> tag. JS 1.1.

lastModified

A read-only string that specifies the date of the most recent change to the document (as reported by the web server). JS 1.0.

linkColor

A string that specifies the color of unvisited links. Deprecated.

links[ ]

An array of Link objects, one for each hypertext link that appears in the document.

location

The URL of the document. Deprecated in favor of the URL property.

plugins[ ]

A synonym for the embeds[ ] array. JS 1.1.

referrer

A read-only string that contains the URL of the document, if any, from which the current document was linked.

title

The text contents of the <title> tag. Read-only prior to DOM Level 1.

URL

A read-only string that specifies the URL of the document. JS 1.1.

vlinkColor

A string that specifies the color of visited links. Deprecated.

W3C DOM Properties

In DOM-compliant browsers, the Document object inherits the properties of Node, and defines the following additional properties.

body

A reference to the Element object that represents the <body> tag of this document.

defaultView

The Window in which the document is displayed. Read-only. DOM Level 2.

documentElement

A read-only reference to the <html> tag of the document.

implementation

The DOMImplementation object that represents the implementation that created this document. Read-only.

IE 4 Properties

The following non-standard (and non-portable) properties are defined by Internet Explorer 4 and later versions.

activeElement
> A read-only property that refers to the input element that is currently active (i.e., has the input focus).

all[ ]
> An array of all Element objects within the document. This array may be indexed numerically to access elements in source order, or it may be indexed by element id or name.

charset
> The character set of the document.

children[ ]
> An array that contains the HTML elements that are direct children of the document. Note that this is different than the all[ ] array that contains all elements in the document, regardless of their position in the containment hierarchy.

defaultCharset
> The default character set of the document.

expando
> This property, if set to false, prevents client-side objects from being expanded. That is, it causes a runtime error if a program attempts to set the value of a nonexistent property of a client-side object. Setting expando to false can sometimes help to catch bugs caused by property misspellings, which can otherwise be difficult to detect. This property can be particularly helpful for programmers who are switching to JavaScript after becoming accustomed to case-insensitive languages. Although expando only works in IE, it can be safely (but ineffectively) set in Netscape.

parentWindow
> The window that contains the document.

readyState
> Specifies the loading status of a document. It has one of the following four string values:

uninitialized
> The document has not started loading.

loading
> The document is loading.

interactive
> The document has loaded sufficiently for the user to interact with it.

complete
> The document is completely loaded.

Netscape 4 Properties

The following non-standard (and non-portable) properties are defined by Netscape 4.

height
> The height, in pixels, of the document.

layers[ ]
> An array of Layer objects that represents the layers contained within a document. This property is only available in Netscape 4; it has been discontinued as of Netscape 6.

width
> The width, in pixels, of the document.

Common Methods

All implementations of the Document object support the following methods. This list is followed by separate lists of methods defined by the W3C DOM standard and by the IE 4 and Netscape 4 Document objects.

clear( )
> Erases the contents of the document and returns nothing. This method is deprecated in JavaScript 1.1. JS 1.0; deprecated.

close( )
> Closes a document stream opened with the open( ) method and returns nothing. JS 1.0.

```
open()
```
Deletes existing document content and opens a stream to which new document contents may be written. Returns nothing. JS 1.0.

```
write(value, ...)
```
Inserts the specified string or strings into the document currently being parsed or appends to document opened with open(). Returns nothing. JS 1.0.

```
writeln(value, ...)
```
Identical to write(), except that it appends a newline character to the output. Returns nothing. JS 1.0

W3C DOM Methods

In DOM-compliant browsers, the Document object inherits the methods of Node, and defines the following additional methods.

```
createAttribute(name)
```
Returns a newly-created Attr node with the specified name.

```
createComment(text)
```
Creates and returns a new Comment node containing the specified text.

```
createDocumentFragment()
```
Creates and returns an empty DocumentFragment node.

```
createElement(tagName)
```
Creates and returns a new Element node with the specified tag name.

```
createTextNode(text)
```
Creates and returns a new Text node that contains the specified text.

```
getElementById(id)
```
Returns the Element of this document that has the specified value for its id attribute, or null if no such Element exists in the document.

```
getElementsByName(name)
```
Returns an array of nodes of all elements in the document that have a specified value for their name attribute. If no such elements are found, returns a zero-length array.

getElementsByTagName(*tagname*)
> Returns an array of all Element nodes in this document that have the specified tag name. The Element nodes appear in the returned array in the same order they appear in the document source.

importNode(*importedNode, deep*)
> Creates and returns a copy of a node from some other document that is suitable for insertion into this document. If the *deep* argument is true, it recursively copies the children of the node too. DOM Level 2.

Netscape 4 Methods

getSelection()
> Returns the currently selected document text with HTML tags removed.

IE 4 Methods

elementFromPoint(x,y)
> Returns the Element located at a specified point.

Event Handlers

In DOM-compliant browsers and IE 4, the Document object supports the same list of generic event handlers that the Element object does. Although the onload and onunload handlers logically belong to the Document object, they are implemented as properties of the Window object.

See Also

Anchor, Applet, Element, Form, Image, Layer, Link, Window

DocumentFragment

DOM Level 1

nodes to be manipulated together

Inherits From: Node

Description

DocumentFragment inherits the methods and properties of Node, and defines no new method or properties of its own. It has one important behavior, however: when a DocumentFragment is inserted into a document tree, it is not the DocumentFragment node itself that is inserted, but the children of the DocumentFragment. This makes DocumentFragment useful as a temporary placeholder for nodes you want to insert, all at once, into a document.

See Also

`Document.createDocumentFragment()`

Element   DOM Level 1, IE 4

an HTML tag in a document   Inherits From: Node (in DOM Level 1)

Description

The Element object represents an HTML element or tag. IE 4 and later, DOM-compliant browsers such as IE 5 and later, and Netscape 6 and later allow access to every element of a document. They also define the properties and methods listed here on each of those elements. Unfortunately, the methods and properties defined by the IE 4 DOM are not the same as the methods and properties defined by the W3C DOM standard. Because of this incompatibility, they are grouped separately in the following lists.

W3C DOM Properties

In web browsers that support the W3C DOM, all elements in an HTML document have properties that correspond to their HTML attributes, including such universal attributes such as dir, id, lang, and title. When an HTML attribute name consists of multiple words, the corresponding JavaScript property name uses mixed case. Otherwise the JavaScript property is in lowercase (e.g., id and href, but tagIndex and accessKey). Two HTML attributes have names that are reserved words in JavaScript or Java, and special property names are required. JavaScript uses the property className to refer to the class attribute of all HTML tags and uses htmlFor to refer to the for attribute of <label> and <script> tags. In addition to their HTML attributes, all elements define the following properties. Remember also that in DOM-compliant browsers, all HTML elements inherit the properties of the Node object.

className

> The string value of the class attribute of the element, which specifies one or more CSS classes. Note that this property is not named "class" because that name is a reserved word in JavaScript.

style

> A Style object that represents the style attribute of the HTML element.

tagName

> The read-only tag name of the element. For HTML documents, the tag name is returned in uppercase, regardless of its capitalization in the document source. In XHTML documents, the value is in lowercase.

IE DOM Properties

Internet Explorer 4 and later versions define a proprietary DOM. In the IE 4 DOM, as in the W3C DOM, each HTML element has JavaScript properties that correspond to its HTML attributes. In addition, the IE 4 DOM defines the following properties for each element:

all[ ]

> An array of all Element objects that are descendants of this element. This array may be indexed numerically to access elements in source order. Or it may be indexed by element id or name. See also Document.all[ ].

children[ ]

> An array of Element objects that are direct children of this element. Note that the IE 4 DOM has no equivalent of the Text or Comment nodes, so the children of an element can only be other Element objects.

className

> A read/write string that specifies the value of the class attribute of an element.

document

> A reference to the containing Document object.

innerHTML

> The HTML text contained within the element, not including the opening and closing tags of the element itself. Setting this

property replaces the content of the element. Because this non-standard property is powerful and widely used, it has been implemented by other browsers including Netscape 6 and later and Mozilla.

innerText

The plain text contained within the element, not including the opening and closing tags of the element itself. Setting this property replaces the content of the element with unparsed plain text.

offsetHeight

The height, in pixels, of the element and all its content.

offsetLeft

The X-coordinate of the element relative to the offsetParent container element.

offsetParent

Specifies the container element that defines the coordinate system in which offsetLeft and offsetTop are measured. For most elements, offsetParent is the Document object that contains them. However, if an element has a dynamically positioned ancestor, that ancestor is the offsetParent. Table cells are positioned relative to the row in which they are contained.

offsetTop

The Y-coordinate of the element, relative to the offsetParent container element.

offsetWidth

The width, in pixels, of the element and all its content.

outerHTML

The HTML text of an element, including its start tags, end tags, and content. Setting this property completely replaces the element and its content.

outerText

The plain text of an element, including its start and end tags. Setting this property replaces the element and its contents with unparsed plain text.

parentElement

> The element that is the direct parent of this one. This property is read-only.

sourceIndex

> The index of the element in the Document.all[] array of the document that contains it.

style

> A Style object that represents the inline CSS style attributes for this element. Setting properties of this object changes the display style of the element.

tagName

> A read-only string that specifies the name of the HTML tag that this element represents.

W3C DOM Methods

In web browsers that support the W3C DOM, all elements in an HTML document support the following methods, and also inherit the methods of Node. Many of these methods are used to get and set attribute values, and are rarely used because Element objects have properties that mirror all their HTML attributes.

getAttribute(name)

> Returns the value of a named attribute as a string.

getAttributeNode(name)

> Returns the value of a named attribute as an Attr node.

getElementsByTagName(name)

> Returns an array of all descendants of this element that have the specified tag name, in the order in which they appear in the document.

hasAttribute(name)

> Returns true if this element has an attribute with the specified name, or false if it does not. DOM Level 2.

removeAttribute(name)

> Deletes the named attribute from this element and returns nothing.

removeAttributeNode(*oldAttr*)

    Removes the specified Attr node from the list of attributes for this element. Returns the Attr node that was removed.

setAttribute(*name, value*)

    Sets the named attribute to the specified string value and returns nothing.

setAttributeNode(*newAttr*)

    Adds the specified Attr node to the list of attributes for this element. If an attribute with the same name already exists, its value is replaced. Returns the Attr node that was replaced by *newAttr*, or null if no attribute was replaced.

IE DOM Methods

Internet Explorer 4 and later versions support the following non-standard methods for all document elements.

contains(*target*)

    Returns true if this element contains the Element *target*, or false if it does not.

getAttribute(*name*)

    Returns the value of the named attribute of this element as a string, or null if there is no such attribute.

insertAdjacentHTML(*where, text*)

    Inserts the HTML *text* into the document near this element at a position specified by *where*. *where* must be one of the strings "BeforeBegin", "AfterBegin", "BeforeEnd" or "AfterEnd". Returns nothing.

insertAdjacentText(*where, text*)

    Inserts plain text *text* into the document near this element, at the position specified by *where*. Returns nothing.

removeAttribute(*name*)

    Deletes the named attribute and its value from the element. Returns true on success; false on failure.

scrollIntoView(*top*)

    Scrolls the document so this element is visible at the top or bottom of the window. If *top* is true or is omitted, the element appears at the top of the window. If false, the element appears at the bottom.

setAttribute(*name*, *value*)

> Sets the named attribute to the specified string value and returns nothing.

Event Handlers

Elements of an HTML document define the following event handlers to respond to raw mouse and keyboard events. Particular types of elements (such as the Form and Input objects) may define more specialized event handlers (such as onsubmit and onchange) that impose an interpretation upon the raw input events.

onclick

> Invoked when the user clicks on the element.

ondblclick

> Invoked when the user double-clicks on the element.

onhelp

> Invoked when the user requests help. IE only.

onkeydown

> Invoked when the user presses a key.

onkeypress

> Invoked when the user presses and releases a key.

onkeyup

> Invoked when the user releases a key.

onmousedown

> Invoked when the user presses a mouse button.

onmousemove

> Invoked when the user moves the mouse.

onmouseout

> Invoked when the user moves the mouse off the element.

onmouseover

> Invoked when the user moves the mouse over an element.

onmouseup

> Invoked when the user releases a mouse button.

See Also

Form, Input, Node, Select, Textarea

Error
Core JavaScript 1.5; JScript 5.5; ECMA v3

predefined exception types
Inherits From: Object

Constructor

```
new Error(message)
new EvalError(message)
new RangeError(message)
new ReferenceError(message)
new SyntaxError(message)
new TypeError(message)
new URIError(message)
```

These constructors create an instance of the Error class or of one of its subclasses. The *message* argument is optional.

Properties

Error and all of its subclasses define the same two properties:

message
>   An error message that provides details about the exception. This property holds the string passed to the constructor, or an implementation-defined default string.

name
>   A string that specifies the type of the exception. This property is always the name of the constructor used to create the exception object.

Methods

toString()
>   Returns a string representation of the Error (or subclass) object.

Event
DOM Level 2, IE 4, Netscape 4

event details

Description

The Event object serves to provide both details about an event and control over the propagation of an event. DOM Level 2 defines a standard Event object, but Internet Explorer 4, 5, and 6 use a proprietary object instead. Netscape 4 has its own proprietary object that is different from the other two. DOM Level 2 does not standardize keyboard events, so the Netscape 4 Event object may be still useful to programmers interested in key events in Netscape 6 and later. The properties of the DOM, IE, and Netscape 4 Event objects are listed in separate sections below.

In the DOM and Netscape event models, an Event object is passed as an argument to the event handler. In the IE event model, the Event object that describes the most recent event is instead stored in the event property of the Window object.

DOM Constants

These constants are the legal values of the eventPhase property; they represent the current phase of event propagation for this event.

Event.CAPTURING_PHASE = 1
> The event is in its capturing phase.

Event.AT_TARGET = 2
> The event is being handled by its target node.

Event.BUBBLING_PHASE = 3
> The event is bubbling.

DOM Properties

All properties of this object are read-only.

altKey
> true if the **Alt** key was held down when an event occurred. Defined for mouse events.

bubbles
> true if the event is of a type that bubbles; false otherwise. Defined for all events.

button
> Specifies which mouse button changed state during a mouse-down, mouseup, or click event. 0 indicates the left button, 1 indicates the middle button, and 2 indicates the right button. Note that this property is only defined when a button changes state: it is not used to report whether a button is held down during a mousemove event, for example. Also, this property is

not a bitmap: it cannot tell you if more than one button is held down. Netscape 6.0 uses the values 1, 2, and 3 instead of 0, 1, and 2. This is fixed in Netscape 6.1.

cancelable

true if the default action associated with the event can be canceled with preventDefault( ), false otherwise. Defined for all events.

clientX, clientY

These properties specify the X and Y coordinates of the mouse pointer, relative to the client area of the browser window. Note that these coordinates do not take document scrolling into account. Defined for mouse events.

ctrlKey

true if the **Ctrl** key was held down when the event occurred. Defined for mouse events.

currentTarget

The document node that is currently handling this event. During capturing and bubbling, this is different than target. Defined for all events.

detail

The click count: 1 for a single click, 2 for a double-click, 3 for a triple click, and so on. Defined for click, mousedown and mouseup events.

eventPhase

The current phase of event propagation. The constants above define the three legal values for this property. Defined for all events.

metaKey

true if the **Meta** key was held down when the event occurred. Defined for mouse events.

relatedTarget

For mouseover events, this is the document node that the mouse left when it moved over the target. For mouseout events, it is the node that the mouse entered when leaving the target. It is undefined for other types of events.

screenX, screenY

These properties specify the X and Y coordinates of the mouse pointer relative to the upper-left corner of the user's screen. Defined for mouse events.

shiftKey

true if the **Shift** key was held down when the event occurred. Defined for mouse events.

target

The target for this event; the document node that generated the event. Note that this may be any node, including Text nodes; it is not restricted to Element nodes. Defined for all events.

timeStamp

A Date object that specifies the date and time at which the event occurred. Defined for all events, but implementations are not required to provide a valid timestamp.

type

The type of event that occurred. This is the name of the event handler property with the leading "on" removed. For example, "click", "load", or "mousedown". Defined for all events.

view

The Window object in which the event was generated.

DOM Methods

preventDefault()

Tells the web browser not to perform the default action (if there is one) associated with this event. If the event is not of a type that is cancelable, this method has no effect. Returns nothing.

stopPropagation()

Stops the event from propagating any further through the capturing, target, or bubbling phases of event propagation. Returns nothing.

IE 4 Properties

altKey

A boolean value that specifies whether the **Alt** key was held down when the event occurred.

button

For mouse events, button specifies which mouse button or buttons were pressed. This read-only integer is a bitmask: the 1 bit is set if the left button was pressed. The 2 bit is set if the right button was pressed. The 4 bit is set if the middle button (of a three button mouse) was pressed.

cancelBubble

If an event handler wants to stop an event from being propagated up to containing objects, it must set this property to true.

clientX, clientY

The X and Y coordinates, relative to the web browser page, at which the event occurred.

ctrlKey

A boolean value that specifies whether the **Ctrl** key was held down when the event occurred.

fromElement

For mouseover and mouseout events, fromElement refers to the object from which the mouse pointer is moving.

keyCode

For keyboard events, keyCode specifies the Unicode character code generated by the key that was struck.

offsetX, offsetY

The X and Y coordinates at which the event occurred, within the coordinate system of the event's source element (see srcElement).

returnValue

If this property is set, its value takes precedence over the value actually returned by an event handler. Set this property to false to cancel the default action of the source element on which the event occurred.

screenX, screenY

> The X and Y coordinates, relative to the screen, at which the event occurred.

shiftKey

> A boolean value that specifies whether the **Shift** key was held down when the event occurred.

srcElement

> The Window, Document, or Element object that generated the event.

toElement

> For mouseover and mouseout events, toElement refers to the object into which the mouse pointer is moving.

type

> A string property that specifies the type of the event. Its value is the name of the event handler, minus the "on" prefix. So, when the onclick() event handler is invoked, the type property of the Event object is "click".

x, y

> The X and Y coordinates at which the event occurred. These properties specify coordinates relative to the innermost containing element that is dynamically positioned using CSS.

Netscape 4 Properties

height

> Set only in resize events. Specifies the new height of the window or frame that was resized.

layerX, layerY

> Specify the X and Y coordinates, relative to the enclosing layer, at which an event occurred.

modifiers

> Specifies which keyboard modifier keys were held down when the event occurred. This numeric value is a bitmask consisting of any of the constants Event.ALT_MASK, Event.CONTROL_MASK, Event.META_MASK, or Event.SHIFT_MASK. Due to a bug, this property is not defined in Netscape 6 or 6.1.

pageX, pageY

> The X and Y coordinates, relative to the web browser page, at which the event occurred. Note that these coordinates are relative to the top-level page, not to any enclosing layers.

screenX, screenY

> The X and Y coordinates, relative to the screen, at which the event occurred.

target

> The Window, Document, Layer, or Element object on which the event occurred.

type

> A string property that specifies the type of the event. Its value is the name of the event handler, minus the "on" prefix. So, when the onclick() event handler is invoked, the type property of the Event object is "click".

which

> For keyboard and mouse events, which specifies which key or mouse button was pressed or released. For keyboard events, this property contains the character encoding of the key that was pressed. For mouse events, it contains 1, 2, or 3, indicating the left, middle, or right buttons.

width

> Set only in resize events. Specifies the new width of the window or frame that was resized.

x, y

> The X and Y coordinates at which the event occurred. These properties are synonyms for layerX and layerY and specify the position relative to the containing layer (if any).

Form   Client-side JavaScript 1.0

an HTML input form   Inherits From: Element

Synopsis

```
document.forms[form_number]
document.forms[form_name]
document.form_name
```

Properties

The Form object defines properties for each of the attributes of the HTML `<form>` element, such as action, encoding, method, name, and target. In addition, it defines the following properties:

elements[ ]
> A read-only array of Input objects representing the elements that appear in the form. The array can be indexed numerically, or by element name for elements that have HTML name attributes defined.

length
> The number of elements in the form. Equivalent to elements.length.

Methods

reset( )
> Resets each of the input elements of the form to their default values. Returns nothing. JS 1.1.

submit( )
> Submits the form, but does not trigger the onsubmit event handler. Returns nothing.

Event Handlers

onreset
> Invoked just before the elements of the form are reset. Return false to prevent reset.

onsubmit
> Invoked just before the form is submitted. This event handler allows form entries to be validated before being submitted. Return false to prevent submission.

See Also

Element, Input, Select, Textarea

Function   Core JavaScript 1.0; JScript 1.0; ECMA v1

a JavaScript function

Constructor

    new Function(argument_names..., body)

This constructor was introduced in JavaScript 1.1, and has been obsoleted by the function literal syntax of JavaScript 1.2.

Properties

length
  The number of named arguments specified when the function was declared. See Arguments.length for the number of argument actually passed. JS 1.1; JScript 2.0; ECMA v1.

prototype
  An object which, for a constructor function, defines properties and methods shared by all objects created with that constructor function. JS 1.1; JScript 2.0; ECMA v1.

Methods

apply(thisobj, args)
  Invokes the function as a method of thisobj, passing the elements of the array args as arguments to the function. Returns whatever value is returned by the invocation of the function. JS 1.2; JScript 5.5; ECMA v3.

call(thisobj, args...)
  Invokes the function as a method of thisobj, using any subsequent arguments as arguments to the function. Returns the value that is returned by the invocation of the function. JS 1.5; JScript 5.5; ECMA v3.

toString()
  Returns a string representation of the function. In some implementations, this is the actual source code of the function. JS 1.0; JScript 2.0; ECMA v1.

See Also

Arguments

Global
Core JavaScript 1.0; JScript 1.0; ECMA v1

global properties and functions

Synopsis

    this

Description

The Global object holds the global properties and methods listed. These properties and methods do not need to be referenced or invoked through any other object. Any variables and functions you define in your own top-level code become properties of the Global object. The Global object has no name, but you can refer to it in top-level code (i.e. outside of methods) with the this keyword. In client-side JavaScript, the Window object serves as the Global object. It has quite a few additional properties and methods, and can be referred to as window.

Global Properties

Infinity
    A numeric value that represents positive infinity. JS 1.3; JScript 3.0; ECMA v1.

NaN
    The not-a-number value. JS 1.3; JScript 3.0; ECMA v1.

undefined
    The undefined value. JS 1.5; JScript 5.5; ECMA v3.

Global Functions

decodeURI(*uri*)
    Returns a decoded copy of *uri*, with any hexadecimal escape sequences replaced with the characters they represent. JS 1.5; JScript 5.5; ECMA v3.

decodeURIComponent(*s*)
    Returns a decoded copy of *s*, with any hexadecimal escape sequences replaced with the characters they represent. JS 1.5; JScript 5.5; ECMA v3.

encodeURI(*uri*)

> Returns an encoded copy of *uri*, with certain characters replaced by hexadecimal escape sequences. Does not encode characters such as #, ? and @ that are used to separate the components of a URI. JS 1.5; JScript 5.5; ECMA v3.

encodeURIComponent(*s*)

> Returns an encoded copy of *s*, with certain characters replaced by hexadecimal escape sequences. Encodes any punctuation characters that could be used to separate components of a URI. JS 1.5; JScript 5.5; ECMA v3.

escape(*s*)

> Returns an encoded copy of *s* in which certain characters have been replaced by hexadecimal escape sequences. JS 1.0; JScript 1.0; ECMA v1; deprecated in ECMA v3; use encodeURI() and encodeURIComponent() instead.

eval(*code*)

> Evaluates a string of JavaScript code and returns the result.

isFinite(*n*)

> Returns true if *n* is (or can be converted to) a finite number. Returns false if *n* is (or converts to) NaN (not a number) or positive or negative infinity. JS 1.2; JScript 3.0; ECMA v1.

isNaN(*x*)

> Returns true if *x* is (or can be converted to) the not-a-number value. Returns false if *x* is (or can be converted to) any numeric value. JS 1.1; JScript 1.0; ECMA v1.

parseFloat(*s*)

> Converts the string *s* (or a prefix of *s*) to a number and returns that number. Returns NaN (0 in JS 1.0) if *s* does not begin with a valid number. JS 1.0; JScript 1.1; ECMA v1.

parseInt(*s*, *radix*)

> Converts the string *s* (or a prefix of *s*) to an integer and returns that integer. Returns NaN (0 in JS 1.0) if *s* does not begin with a valid number. The optional *radix* argument specifies the radix (between 2 and 36) to use. If omitted, base 10 is the default or base 16 if *s* begins with the hexadecimal prefix "0x" or "0X". JS 1.0; JScript 1.1; ECMA v1.

unescape(s)

> Decodes a string encoded with escape(). Returns a decoded copy of s. JS 1.0; JScript 1.0; ECMA v1; deprecated in ECMA v3; use decodeURI() and decodeURIComponent() instead.

See Also

Window

History

go back or forward in browsing history

Synopsis

```
window.history
history
```

Methods

back()

> Goes back to a previously visited URL in the browsing history. Returns nothing.

forward()

> Goes forward in the browsing history. Returns nothing.

go(n)

> Goes to the nth URL relative to the currently displayed URL. Calling this method with -1 is the same as calling the back() method. Returns nothing.

Image

an HTML image

Inherits From: Element

Synopsis

```
document.images[i]
document.images[image-name]
document.image-name
```

Constructor

```
new Image(width, height);
```

This constructor creates an off-screen Image object that cannot be displayed. The *width* and *height* arguments are optional. Setting the src attribute of the resulting object causes the browser to preload an image into its cache.

Properties

The Image object defines properties for each of the attributes of the HTML <img> element, such as src, border, width, height, vspace, and hspace. In addition, it defines or provides special behavior for the following properties:

complete
> false if the image is still loading. true if it has finished loading or if there was an error while loading. Read-only.

src
> A read/write string that specifies the URL of the image to be displayed by the browser. This property simply mirrors the src attribute of the <img> tag, but is detailed here because many important DHTML effects are created by dynamically setting the src property of an Image object, to replace one image with another.

Event Handlers

Image inherits event handlers from Element and also defines the following:

onabort
> Invoked if the user aborts the download of an image.

onerror
> Invoked if an error occurs while downloading the image.

onload
> Invoked when the image successfully finishes loading.

Input

a form input element

Inherits From: Element

Synopsis

```
form.elements[i]
form.elements[name]
form.name
```

Properties

The Input object defines properties for each of the attributes of the HTML <input> tag, such as maxLength, readOnly, size, and tabIndex. In addition, it defines the following properties:

checked

A read/write boolean that specifies whether an input element of type "checkbox" or "radio" is checked (true) or not (false).

defaultChecked

A boolean that specifies whether an input element of type "checkbox" or "radio" is checked when first created or when it is reset to its initial state.

defaultValue

A string that specifies the text that appears in an input element of type "text" or "password" when it is first created or when it is reset to its initial state. For security reasons, this property does not affect input elements of type file.

form

A read-only reference to the Form object that contains the element. This property is defined for input elements of all types.

name

The name of this input element, as specified by the HTML name attribute. This property is defined for input elements of all types.

type

A string that specifies the type of the form element. This property mirrors the HTML type attribute. Legal values are listed in the following table; the default is text. Submit and

Textarea objects also have a type property, with possible values select-one, select-multiple, and textarea. JS 1.1.

Type	Description
"button"	Push button
"checkbox"	Checkbox element
"file"	File upload element
"hidden"	Hidden element
"image"	Graphical form submit button
"password"	Masked text entry field
"radio"	Mutually-exclusive radio button
"reset"	Form reset button
"text"	Single-line text entry field
"submit"	Form submission button

value

The string value that is sent when the form is submitted. For input elements of type "text", "password", and "file", this is the editable text displayed in the element. You can set this property to change that displayed text. For input elements of type "button", "submit", and "reset", value is the label that appears in the button. For other types, the value string is not displayed. Note that for security reasons, the value property of elements of type "file" is usually read-only.

Methods

blur( )

Yields the keyboard focus and returns nothing. Defined for all element types except "hidden".

click( )

Simulates a mouse click on the form element and returns nothing. Defined for button element types: "button", "checkbox", "radio", "reset", and "submit".

focus()

Takes the keyboard focus and returns nothing. Defined for all element types except "hidden".

select()

Selects the text that appears in the element and returns nothing. Works for elements of type "text", "password", and "file". Also defined by the Textarea object.

Event Handlers

onblur

Invoked when the element loses keyboard focus. Defined for all element types except "hidden".

onchange

For text-entry elements of type "text", "password", and "file", this event handler is invoked when the user changes the displayed text and then transfers keyboard focus away from the element, signaling that text entry is complete. It is not invoked for each keystroke.

onclick

For button elements of type "button", "checkbox", "radio", "reset", and "submit", this event handler is invoked when the user clicks the button. Return false to prevent form submission or reset for elements of type "submit" and "reset", respectively.

onfocus

Invoked the element gains keyboard focus. Defined for all element types except "hidden".

See Also

Form, Option, Select, Textarea

Layer   Client-side Netscape 4 only

An independent document layer

Synopsis

```
document.layers[i]
document.layers[layer-name]
document.layer-name
```

Constructor

```
new Layer(width, parent_layer)
```

Description

The Layer object is supported only in Netscape 4 and was discontinued in Netscape 6. It is entirely non-standard, but is documented here because it provides the only way to work with dynamically positioned objects in Netscape 4. Any HTML element with a CSS position attribute of absolute is represented by a Layer object in JavaScript. You can also create layers with the non-standard <layer> tag, or with the Layer() constructor.

Properties

above
> The layer above this one, if any. Read-only.

background
> The background image of the layer.

below
> The layer below this one, if any. Read-only.

bgColor
> The background color of the layer.

clip.bottom
> The Y-coordinate of the bottom edge of the layer's clipping area, relative to top.

clip.height
> The height of the layer's clipping area. Setting this property also sets the value of clip.bottom.

clip.left
> The X-coordinate of the left edge of the layer's clipping area, relative to left.

clip.right
> The X-coordinate of the right edge of the layer's clipping area, relative to left.

clip.top
> The Y-coordinate of the top edge of the layer's clipping area, relative to top.

clip.width

The width of the layer's clipping area. Setting this property also sets the value of clip.right.

document

A read-only reference to the Document object contained within the layer.

hidden

Specifies whether a layer is hidden or visible. Setting this property to true hides the layer, and setting it to false makes the layer visible.

layers[ ]

An array that contains any child Layer objects of this layer. It is the same as the document.layers[ ] array of a layer.

left

The X-coordinate of this layer, relative to the containing layer or document. Setting this property moves the layer to the left or right. left is a synonym for x.

name

The name attribute of the HTML tag represented by this layer.

pageX, pageY

The X and Y-coordinates of this layer relative to the top-level document. Note that these coordinates are relative to the top-level page, not relative to any containing layer.

parentLayer

A read-only reference to the Layer or Window object that contains (is the parent of) this layer.

siblingAbove, siblingBelow

These properties refer to the sibling Layer object (i.e., a child of the same parent Layer) immediately above or below this layer in the stacking order. If there is no such layer, these properties are null.

src

A read/write string that specifies the URL, if any, of the contents of a layer. Setting this property to a new URL causes the browser to read the contents of that URL and display them in the layer.

top

The Y-coordinate of this layer relative to the containing layer or document. Setting this property moves the layer up or down. top is a synonym for y.

visibility

A read/write string that specifies the visibility of the layer. The three legal values are: "show", "hide", and "inherit".

window

The Window object that contains the layer, regardless of how deeply nested the layer is within other layers.

x, y

The X and Y-coordinates of the layer. x is a synonym for the left property and y is a synonym for the top property.

zIndex

The position of the layer in the z-order, or stacking order, of layers. When two layers overlap, the one with the higher zIndex appears on top and obscures the one with the lower zIndex. If two sibling layers have the same zIndex, the one that appears later in the layers[] array of the containing document is displayed later and overlaps the one that appears earlier.

Methods

load(src, width)

Loads a new URL into the layer, sets the layer width, and returns nothing.

moveAbove(other_layer)

Moves this layer above another and returns nothing.

moveBelow(other_layer)

Moves this layer below another and returns nothing.

moveBy(dx, dy)

Moves the layer relative to its current position and returns nothing.

moveTo(x, y)

Moves the layer to the point (x,y) relative to its containing layer or window and returns nothing.

moveToAbsolute(*x, y*)

Moves the layer to a position relative to the page and returns nothing.

resizeBy(*dw, dh*)

Resizes the layer by the specified amounts and returns nothing.

resizeTo(*width, height*)

Resizes the layer to the specified size returns nothing.

Link

an <a> or <area> link   Inherits From: Element

Synopsis

> *document*.links[*i*]

Properties

Many of the properties of a Link object represent portions of its URL. For each such property below, the example given is a portion of the following (fictitious) URL:

```
http://www.oreilly.com:1234/catalog/search.html
?q=JavaScript&m=10#results
```

hash

A read/write string property that specifies the anchor portion of the Link's URL, including the leading hash (#) mark. For example: "#result".

host

A read/write string property that specifies the hostname and port portions of a Link's URL. For example: "www.oreilly.com:1234".

hostname

A read/write string property that specifies the hostname portion of a Link's URL. For example: "www.oreilly.com".

href

A read/write string property that specifies the complete text of the Link's URL.

pathname

> A read/write string property that specifies the pathname portion of a Link's URL. For example: "/catalog/search.html".

port

> A read/write string (not a number) property that specifies the port portion of a Link's URL. For example: "1234".

protocol

> A read/write string property that specifies the protocol portion of a Link's URL, including the trailing colon. For example: "http:".

search

> A read/write string property that specifies the query portion of a Link's URL, including the leading question mark. For example: "?q=JavaScript&m=10".

target

> A read/write string property that specifies the name of a Window object (i.e., a frame or a top-level browser window) in which the linked document should be displayed. This property is the standard target HTML attribute. The special names "_blank", "_top", "_parent", and "_self" are allowed.

Event Handlers

onclick

> Invoked when the user clicks on the link. In JavaScript 1.1, this event handler may prevent the link from being followed by returning false.

onmouseout

> Invoked when the user moves the mouse off the link. JS 1.1.

onmouseover

> Invoked when the user moves the mouse over the link. The status property of the current window may be set here. Return true to tell the browser not to display the URL of the link in the status line.

See Also

Anchor, Location

Location

current browser location

Synopsis

```
location
window.location
```

Properties

The Location object defines the same URL-related properties that the Link object does, with the exception of the target. See the Link object for a description of the hash, host, hostname, href, pathname, port, protocol, and search properties. Setting any of these properties causes the browser to load and display the document from the new URL. As a shortcut, you can also load a new document by assigning a URL string to the location property of the Window.

Methods

reload(*force*)

Reloads the current document from the cache or the server. The *force* argument is optional. If true, it forces a complete reload, even if the document has not been modified. Returns nothing. JS 1.1.

replace(*url*)

Replaces the current document with a new one, without generating a new entry in the browsing history. Returns nothing. JS 1.1.

See Also

Link, Window.location

Math

mathematical functions and constants

Synopsis

```
Math.constant
Math.function()
```

Description

The Math object is a placeholder for grouping mathematical constants and functions. It does not define a class of objects as Date and String do. There is no Math() constructor, and functions like Math.sin() are simply functions, not methods that operate on an object.

Constants

Math.E
> The constant e, the base of the natural logarithm.

Math.LN10
> The natural logarithm of 10.

Math.LN2
> The natural logarithm of 2.

Math.LOG10E
> The base-10 logarithm of e.

Math.LOG2E
> The base-2 logarithm of e.

Math.PI
> The constant π.

Math.SQRT1_2
> 1 divided by the square root of 2.

Math.SQRT2
> The square root of 2.

Functions

Math.abs(x)
> Returns the absolute value of x.

Math.acos(x)
> Returns the arc cosine of x; the return value is between 0 and π radians.

Math.asin(x)
> Returns the arc sine of x; the return value is between $-\pi/2$ and $\pi/2$ radians.

`Math.atan(x)`

> Returns the arc tangent of x; the return value is between -π/2 and π/2 radians.

`Math.atan2(y, x)`

> Returns a value between -π and π radians that specifies the counterclockwise angle between the positive X-axis and the point (x, y). Note the order of the arguments to this function.

`Math.ceil(x)`

> Returns the nearest integer greater than or equal to x.

`Math.cos(x)`

> Returns the cosine of the specified value x.

`Math.exp(x)`

> Returns the constant e raised to the power of x.

`Math.floor(x)`

> Returns the nearest integer less than or equal to x.

`Math.log(x)`

> Returns the natural logarithm of x.

`Math.max(args...)`

> Returns the largest of the arguments. Returns -Infinity if there are no arguments. Returns NaN if any of the arguments is NaN or is a non-numeric value that cannot be converted to a number. Prior to ECMA v3, this function requires exactly 2 arguments.

`Math.min(args...)`

> Returns the smallest of the arguments. Returns Infinity if there are no arguments. Returns NaN if any argument is NaN or is a non-numeric value that cannot be converted to a number. Prior to ECMA v3, this function requires exactly 2 arguments.

`Math.pow(x, y)`

> Returns x to the power of y.

`Math.random( )`

> Returns a pseudo-random number between 0.0 and 1.0. JS 1.1; JScript 1.0; ECMA v1.

`Math.round(x)`

> Returns the integer closest to x.

```
Math.sin(x)
```
Returns the sine of x.

```
Math.sqrt(x)
```
Returns the square root of x. Returns NaN if x is less than zero.

```
Math.tan(x)
```
Returns the tangent of x.

See Also

Number

Navigator   Client-side JavaScript 1.0

information about the browser

Synopsis

```
navigator
```

Properties

appCodeName

A read-only string that specifies a nickname for the browser. In all Netscape browsers, this is "Mozilla". For compatibility, this property is "Mozilla" in Microsoft browsers as well.

appName

A read-only string property that specifies the name of the browser. For Netscape, the value of this property is "Netscape". In IE, the value of this property is "Microsoft Internet Explorer".

appVersion

A read-only string that specifies version and platform information for the browser. The first part of this string is a version number. Pass the string to parseInt() to obtain the major version number only or to parseFloat() to obtain the major and minor version numbers as a floating-point value. The remainder of the string value of this property provides other details about the browser version, including the operating system it is running on. Unfortunately, however, the format of this information varies widely from browser to browser.

---

cookieEnabled

A read-only boolean that is true if the browser has cookies enabled, and false if they are disabled. IE 4, Netscape 6.

language

A read-only string that specifies the default language of the browser version. The value of this property is a standard two-letter language code such as "en" for English or "fr" for French. It can also be a five-letter string indicating a language and a regional variant, such as "fr_CA" for French, as spoken in Canada. Netscape 4; note that IE 4 provides two different language-related properties.

platform

A read-only string that specifies the operating system and/or hardware platform the browser is running under. Although there is not standard set of values for this property, some typical values are "Win32", "MacPPC", and "Linux i586". JS 1.2.

systemLanguage

A read-only string that specifies the default language of the operating system using the same standard codes used by the Netscape-specific language property. IE 4.

userAgent

A read-only string that specifies the value the browser uses for the user-agent header in HTTP requests. Typically, this is the value of navigator.appCodeName followed by a slash and the value of navigator.appVersion.

userLanguage

A read-only string that specifies the preferred language of the user using the same standard codes used by the Netscape-specific language property. IE 4.

Methods

javaEnabled()

Returns true if Java is supported and enabled in the current browser, or false if it is not. JS 1.1.

See Also

Screen

Node

a node in a document tree

Subclasses

Attr, Comment, Document, DocumentFragment, Element, Text

Constants

All nodes in an HTML document are instances of one of the Node subclasses listed above. Every Node object has a nodeType property that specifies which of the subclasses it is an instance of. The following constants are the legal values for nodeType. Note that these are static properties of Node, not properties of individual Node objects. They are not defined in Internet Explorer 4, 5, or 6; in those browsers you must use the corresponding integer literals.

```
Node.ELEMENT_NODE = 1;           // Element
Node.ATTRIBUTE_NODE = 2;         // Attr
Node.TEXT_NODE = 3;              // Text
Node.COMMENT_NODE = 8;           // Comment
Node.DOCUMENT_NODE = 9;          // Document
Node.DOCUMENT_FRAGMENT_NODE=11;  // DocumentFragment
```

Properties

attributes[ ]

> If this Node is an Element, the attributes property is a read-only array of Attr objects that represent the attributes of the element. The array can be indexed by number or by attribute name. All HTML attributes have corresponding Element properties, however, so it is uncommon to use the attributes[ ] array.

childNodes[ ]

> This read-only array of Node objects contains the children of this node. If the node has no children, this property is a zero-length array.

firstChild

> This read-only property refers to the first child Node of this node, or null if the node has no children.

lastChild

> This read-only property refers to the last child Node of this node, or null if the node has no children.

nextSibling

> The sibling Node that immediately follows this one in the childNodes[] array of the parentNode, or null if there is no such node. Read-only.

nodeName

> The name of the node. For Element nodes, this property specifies the tag name of the element, which can also be retrieved with the tagName property of Element. For Attr nodes, this property specifies the attribute name. For other types of nodes, the value is a constant string that specifies the node type. Read-only.

nodeType

> The type of the node. The legal values for this property are defined by the constants listed above.

nodeValue

> The string value of a node. For Text and Comment nodes, this property holds the text content. For Attr nodes, it holds the attribute value. This property is read/write.

ownerDocument

> The Document object of which this Node is a part. For Document nodes, this property is null. Read-only.

parentNode

> The parent or container Node of this node, or null if there is no parent. Note that Document and Attr nodes never have parent nodes. Nodes that have been removed from the document or are newly created and have not yet been inserted into the document tree have a parentNode of null. Read-only.

previousSibling

> The sibling Node that immediately precedes this one in the childNodes[] array of the parentNode, or null, if there is no such node.

Methods

addEventListener(*type, listener, useCapture*)

Registers an event listener for this node. *type* is a string that specifies the event type minus the "on" prefix (e.g., "click" or "submit"). *listener* is the event handler function. When triggered, it is invoked with an Event object as its argument. If *useCapture* is true, this is a capturing event handler. If false or omitted, it is a regular event handler. Returns nothing. DOM Level 2; not supported in IE 4, 5, or 6.

appendChild(*newChild*)

Adds the *newChild* Node to the document tree by appending it to the childNodes[ ] array of this node. If the node is already in the document tree, it is first removed before being reinserted at its new position. Returns the *newChild* argument.

cloneNode(*deep*)

Returns a copy of this node. If deep is true, the descendents of the node are recursively copied as well.

hasAttributes( )

Returns true if this node is an Element and has any attributes. DOM Level 2.

hasChildNodes( )

Returns true if this node has any children.

insertBefore(*newChild, refChild*)

Inserts the *newChild* Node into the document tree immediately before the *refChild* Node, which must be a child of this node. If the node being inserted is already in the tree, it is first removed. Returns *newChild*.

isSupported(*feature, version*)

Returns true if the specified version number of a named feature is supported by this node. See also DOMImplementation. hasFeature( ). DOM Level 2.

normalize( )

Normalizes all Text node descendants of this node by deleting empty Text nodes and merging adjacent Text nodes. Returns nothing.

removeChild(*oldChild*)

> Removes the *oldChild* Node from the document tree. *oldChild* must be a child of this node. Returns oldChild.

removeEventListener(*type, listener, useCapture*)

> Removes the specified event listener. Returns nothing. DOM Level 2; not supported in IE 4, 5, or 6.

replaceChild(*newChild, oldChild*)

> Replaces the *oldChild* Node (which must be a child of this node) with the *newChild* Node. If *newChild* is already in the document tree, it is first removed from its current location. Returns *oldChild*.

See Also

Attr, Comment, Document, DocumentFragment, Element, Text

Number   Core JavaScript 1.1; JScript 2.0; ECMA v1

support for numbers

Constructor

    new Number(*value*)
    Number(*value*)

With the new operator, the Number() constructor converts its argument to a numeric value and returns a new Number object wrapped around that value. Without new, Number() is a conversion function that converts its argument to a number and returns that value.

Constants

These constants are properties of Number itself, not of individual Number objects.

Number.MAX_VALUE

> The largest representable number. Approximately 1.79E+308.

Number.MIN_VALUE

> The smallest representable positive number. Approximately 5E-324.

Number.NaN

> Not-a-number value. Same as the global NaN.

Number.NEGATIVE_INFINITY
> Negative infinite value.

Number.POSITIVE_INFINITY
> Infinite value. Same as global Infinity.

Methods

toExponential(*digits*)
> Returns a string representation of the number, in exponential notation, with one digit before the decimal place and *digits* digits after the decimal place. The fractional part of the number is rounded, or padded with zeros so that it has the specified length. *digits* must be between 0 and 20, and if omitted, as many digits as necessary are used. JS 1.5; JScript 5.5; ECMA v3.

toFixed(*digits*)
> Returns a string representation of the number that does not use exponential notation, and has exactly *digits* digits after the decimal place. *digits* must be between 0 and 20. The number is rounded or padded with zeros if necessary. JS 1.5; JScript 5.5; ECMA v3.

toLocaleString()
> Returns an implementation-dependent string representation of the number, formatted according to local conventions. This may affect things such as the punctuation characters used for the decimal point and the thousands separator. JS 1.5; JScript 5.5; ECMA v3.

toPrecision(*precision*)
> Returns a string representation of *number* that contains *precision* significant digits. *precision* must be between 1 and 21. The returned string uses fixed-point notation where possible, or exponential notation otherwise. The number is rounded or padded with zeros if necessary. JS 1.5; JScript 5.5; ECMA v3.

toString(*radix*)
> Converts a number to a string, using a specified radix (base), and returns the string. *radix* must be between 2 and 36. If omitted, base 10 is used.

See Also

Math

Object

the superclass of all JavaScript objects

Constructor

```
new Object();
```

This constructor creates an empty object to which you can add arbitrary properties.

Properties

All JavaScript objects, how ever they are created, have the following properties.

constructor
A reference to the JavaScript function that was the constructor for the object. JS 1.1; JScript 2.0; ECMA v1.

Methods

All JavaScript objects, how ever they are created, have the following methods.

hasOwnProperty(*propname*)
Returns true if the object has a non-inherited property with the specified name. Returns false if the object does not have a property with the specified name, or if it inherits that property from its prototype object. JS 1.5; JScript 5.5; ECMA v3.

isPrototypeOf(*o*)
Returns true if this object is the prototype of *o*. Returns false if *o* is not an object or if this object is not its prototype. JS 1.5; JScript 5.5; ECMA v3.

propertyIsEnumerable(*propname*)
Returns true if this object has a non-inherited enumerable property with the specified name, and returns false otherwise. Enumerable properties are those that are enumerated by for/in loops. JS 1.5; JScript 5.5; ECMA v3.

toLocaleString()

> Returns a localized string representation of the object. The default implementation of this method simply calls toString( ), but subclasses may override it to provide localization. JS 1.5; JScript 5.5; ECMA v3.

toString()

> Returns a string representation of the object. The implementation of this method provided by the Object class is quite generic and does not provide much useful information. Subclasses of Object typically override this method by defining their own toString() method that produces more useful output. JS 1.0; JScript 2.0; ECMA v1.

valueOf()

> Returns the primitive value of the object, if any. For objects of type Object, this method simply returns the object itself. Subclasses of Object, such as Number and Boolean, override this method to return the primitive value associated with the object. JS 1.1; JScript 2.0; ECMA v1.

See Also

Array, Boolean, Function, Number, String

Option   Client-side JavaScript 1.0

a selectable option   Inherits From: Element

Synopsis

```
select.options[i]
```

Constructor

In JavaScript 1.1 and later, Option objects can be created dynamically with the Option( ) constructor:

```
new Option(text, value, defaultSelected, selected)
```

Properties

defaultSelected

A read/write boolean that specifies whether the option is initially selected when the Select object that contains it is created or reset.

index

A read-only integer that specifies the index of the option within the options[ ] array of the Select object that contains it.

selected

A read/write boolean value that specifies whether an option is currently selected. You can use this property to test whether a given option is selected. You can also set it to select or deselect an option. Note that when you select or deselect an option in this way, the Select.onchange( ) event handler is not invoked.

text

A read/write string that specifies the text that appears to the user for the option.

value

A read/write string that specifies the text that is passed to the web server if the option is selected when the form is submitted.

See Also

Select

RegExp   Core JavaScript 1.2; JScript 3.0; ECMA v3

regular expressions for pattern matching

Literal Syntax

    /pattern/attributes

Constructor

    new RegExp(pattern, attributes)

Regular expression patterns are expressed using a complex grammar that is summarized earlier in this book.

Instance Properties

global

> A read-only boolean that specifies whether the RegExp has the g attribute and therefore performs global matching.

ignoreCase

> A read-only boolean that specifies whether the RegExp has the i attribute and therefore performs case-insensitive matching.

lastIndex

> For global RegExp objects, this read/write property specifies the character position immediately following the last match; this is the first character examined for the next match.

multiline

> A read-only boolean that specifies whether the RegExp has the m attribute and therefore performs multi-line matching.

source

> A read-only string that holds the source text of the regular expression *pattern*, excluding slashes and attributes.

Methods

exec(*string*)

> Matches *string* against this RegExp and returns an array containing the results of the match, or null if no match was found. Element 0 of the array is the matching text. Subsequent elements of the array contain the substrings that matched the subexpressions within the RegExp. The returned array also has an index property that specifies the start position of the match.

test(*string*)

> Returns true if *string* contains text matching this RegExp, or false otherwise.

See Also

String.match( ), String.replace( ), String.search( )

Screen

information about the display   Inherits From:

Synopsis

    screen

Properties

availHeight
> The available height, in pixels, of the screen.

availWidth
> Specifies the available width, in pixels, of the screen.

colorDepth
> The depth of the browser's color palette, or the number of
> bits-per-pixel for the screen.

height
> Specifies the total height, in pixels, of the screen.

width
> Specifies the total width, in pixels, of the screen.

See Also

Navigator

Select

a graphical selection list   Inherits From: Element

Synopsis

    form.elements[i]
    form.elements[element_name]
    form.element_name

Properties

The Select object defines properties for each of the attributes of
the HTML <select> tag, such as disabled, multiple, name, and
size. In addition, it defines the following properties:

form

>   The Form object that contains this Select object. Read-only.

length

>   A read-only integer that specifies the number of elements in the options[ ] array. The value of this property is the same as options.length.

options[ ]

>   An array of Option objects, each describing one of the options displayed within the Select element. You can shorten the set of options by setting the options.length property to a smaller value (or remove all options by setting it to zero). You can remove individual options by setting an element of the array to null—this shifts the elements above it down, shortening the array. You can append options to the Select object by using the Option( ) constructor to create a new Option and assigning it to options[options.length].

selectedIndex

>   A read/write integer that specifies the index of the selected option within the Select object. If no option is selected, selectedIndex is -1. If more than one option is selected, selectedIndex specifies the index of the first one only. Setting this property causes all other options to become deselected. Setting it to -1 causes all options to be deselected.

type

>   A read-only string property that specifies the type of the element. If the Select object allows only a single selection (i.e., if the multiple attribute does not appear in the object's HTML definition), this property is "select-one". Otherwise, the value is "select-multiple". See also Input.type. JS 1.1.

Methods

add(*new, old*)

>   Inserts the Option object *new* into the options[ ] array at the position immediately before the Option object *old*. If *old* is null, the *new* Option is appended to the array. Returns nothing. DOM Level 1.

blur( )

>   Yields the keyboard focus and returns nothing.

focus()
    Grabs the keyboard focus and returns nothing.

remove(n)
    Removes the nth element from the options[] array. Returns
    nothing. DOM Level 1.

Event Handlers

onblur
    Invoked when input focus is lost.

onchange
    Invoked when the user selects or deselects an item.

onfocus
    Invoked when input focus is gained.

See Also

Form, Input, Option

String   Core JavaScript 1.0; JScript 1.0; ECMA v1

string manipulation   Inherits From: Object

Constructor

    String(s)
    new String(s)

Without the new operator, the String() function converts its argument to a string. With the new operator, it is a constructor that
wraps the converted value in a String object.

Properties

length
    The number of characters in the string. Read-only.

Methods

charAt(n)
    Returns the character at position n in the string.

charCodeAt(*n*)

> Returns the Unicode encoding of the character at position *n* in the string. JS 1.2; JScript 5.5; ECMA v1.

concat(*value*, ...)

> Returns a new string that results from converting each of the arguments to a string and concatenating the resulting strings. JS 1.2; JScript 3.0; ECMA v3.

indexOf(*substring*, *start*)

> Returns the position of the first occurrence of *substring* within this string that appears at or after the *start* position or -1 if no such occurrence is found. If *start* is omitted, 0 is used.

lastIndexOf(*substring*, *start*)

> Returns the position of the last occurrence of *substring* within *string* that appears before the *start* position, or -1 if no such occurrence is found. If *start* is omitted, the string length is used.

match(*regexp*)

> Matches this string against the specified regular expression and returns an array containing the match results or null if no match is found. If *regexp* is not a global regular expression, the returned array is the same as for the RegExp.exec() method. If *regexp* is global (has the "g" attribute), the elements of the returned array contain the text of each match found. JS 1.2; JScript 3.0; ECMA v3.

replace(*regexp*, *replacement*)

> Returns a new string, with text matching *regexp* replaced with *replacement*. *regexp* may be a regular expression or a plain string. *replacement* may be a string, containing optional regular expression escape sequences (such as $1) that are replaced with portions of the matched text. It may also be a function that computes the replacement string based on match details passed as arguments. JS 1.2; JScript 3.0; ECMA v3.

search(*regexp*)

> Returns the position of the start of the first substring of this string that matches *regexp*, or -1 if no match was found. JS 1.2; JScript 3.0; ECMA v3.

slice(*start, end*)

Returns a new string that contains all the characters of *string* from and including the position *start* and up to but not including *end*. If *end* is omitted, the slice extends to the end of the string. Negative arguments specify character positions measured from the end of the string. JS 1.2; JScript 3.0; ECMA v3.

split(*delimiter, limit*)

Returns an array of strings, created by splitting *string* into substrings at the boundaries specified by *delimiter*. *delimiter* may be a string or a RegExp. If *delimiter* is a RegExp with a parenthesized subexpression, the delimiter text that matches the subexpression is included in the returned array. See also Array.join( ). JS 1.1; JScript 3.0; ECMA v1.

substring(*from, to*)

Returns a new string that contains characters copied from positions *from* to *to-1* of *string*. If to is omitted, the substring extends to the end of the string. Negative arguments are not allowed.

substr(*start, length*)

Returns a copy of the portion of this string starting at *start* and continuing for *length* characters, or to the end of the string, if *length* is not specified. JS 1.2; JScript 3.0; Non-standard: use slice( ) or substring( ) instead.

toLowerCase( )

Returns a copy of the string, with all uppercase letters converted to their lowercase equivalent, if they have one.

toUpperCase( )

Returns a copy of the string, with all lowercase letters converted to their uppercase equivalent, if they have one.

Static Functions

String.fromCharCode(*c1, c2, ...*)

Returns a new string containing characters with the encodings specified by the numeric arguments. JS 1.2; JScript 3.0; ECMA v1.

Style   DOM Level 2; IE 4

inline CSS properties of an element   Inherits From:

Synopsis

element.style

Properties

The Style object defines a large number of properties: one property for each CSS attribute defined by the CSS2 specification. The property names correspond closely to the CSS attribute names, with minor changes required to avoid syntax errors in JavaScript. Multiword attributes that contain hyphens, such as font-family are written without hyphens in JavaScript, and each word after the first is capitalized: fontFamily. Also, the float attribute conflicts with the reserved word float, so it translates to the property cssFloat.

The visual CSS properties are listed in the following table. Since the properties correspond directly to CSS attributes, no individual documentation is given for each property. See a CSS reference (such as *Cascading Style Sheets: The Definitive Guide* (O'Reilly), by Eric A. Meyer) for the meaning and legal values of each. Note that current browsers do not implement all of these properties.

All of the properties are strings, and care is required when working with properties that have numeric values. When querying such a property, you must use parseFloat() to convert the string to a number. When setting such a property you must convert your number to a string, which you can usually do by adding the required units specification, such as "px".

background	counterIncrement	orphans
backgroundAttachment	counterReset	outline
backgroundColor	cssFloat	outlineColor
backgroundImage	cursor	outlineStyle
backgroundPosition	direction	outlineWidth
backgroundRepeat	display	overflow
border	emptyCells	padding
borderBottom	font	paddingBottom
borderBottomColor	fontFamily	paddingLeft
borderBottomStyle	fontSize	paddingRight
borderBottomWidth	fontSizeAdjust	paddingTop

borderCollapse	fontStretch	page
borderColor	fontStyle	pageBreakAfter
borderLeft	fontVariant	pageBreakBefore
borderLeftColor	fontWeight	pageBreakInside
borderLeftStyle	height	position
borderLeftWidth	left	quotes
borderRight	letterSpacing	right
borderRightColor	lineHeight	size
borderRightStyle	listStyle	tableLayout
borderRightWidth	listStyleImage	textAlign
borderSpacing	listStylePosition	textDecoration
borderStyle	listStyleType	textIndent
borderTop	margin	textShadow
borderTopColor	marginBottom	textTransform
borderTopStyle	marginLeft	top
borderTopWidth	marginRight	unicodeBidi
borderWidth	marginTop	verticalAlign
bottom	markerOffset	visibility
captionSide	marks	whiteSpace
clear	maxHeight	widows
clip	maxWidth	width
color	minHeight	wordSpacing
content	minWidth	zIndex

Text

DOM Level 1

a run of text in a document

Inherits From: Node

Description

A Text object represents a run of plain text without markup in a DOM document tree. Do not confuse it with the single-line text input element of HTML, which is represented by the Input object.

Properties

data

The string of text contained by this node.

length

The number of characters contained by this node. Read-only.

Methods

appendData(*text*)
> Appends the specified *text* to this node and returns nothing.

deleteData(*offset, count*)
> Deletes text from this node, starting with the character at the specified *offset*, and continuing for *count* characters. Returns nothing.

insertData(*offset, text*)
> Inserts the specified *text* into this node at the specified character *offset*. Returns nothing.

replaceData(*offset, count, text*)
> Replaces the characters starting at the specified *offset* and continuing for *count* characters with the specified *text*. Returns nothing.

splitText(*offset*)
> Splits this Text node into two at the specified character position, inserts the new Text node into the document after the original, and returns the new node.

substringData(*offset, count*)
> Returns a string that consists of the *count* characters starting with the character at position *offset*.

See Also

Node.normalize( )

Textarea   Client-side JavaScript 1.0

multiline text input   Inherits From: Element

Synopsis

```
form.elements[i]
form.elements[name]
form.name
```

Description

The Textarea object is very similar to the Input object.

Properties

The Textarea object defines properties for each of the attributes of the HTML <textarea> tag, such as cols, defaultValue, disabled, name, readOnly, and rows. It also defines the following properties:

form

> The Form object that contains this Textarea object. Read-only.

type

> A read-only string property that specifies the type of the element. For Textarea objects, this is always "textarea".

value

> A read/write string that specifies the text contained in the Textarea. The initial value of this property is the same as the defaultValue property.

Methods

blur( )

> Yields the keyboard focus and returns nothing.

focus( )

> Grabs the keyboard focus and returns nothing.

select( )

> Selects the entire contents of the text area. Returns nothing.

Event Handlers

onblur

> Invoked when input focus is lost.

onchange

> Invoked when the user changes the value in the Textarea element and moves the keyboard focus elsewhere. This event handler is invoked only when the user completes an edit in the Textarea element.

onfocus

> Invoked when input focus is gained.

See Also

Element, Form, Input

Window

browser window or frame

Synopsis

```
self
window
window.frames[i]
```

Properties

The Window object defines the following properties. Non-portable, browser-specific properties are listed separately after this list. Note that the Window object is the Global object for client-side JavaScript; therefore the Window object also has the properties listed on the Global reference page.

closed
> A read-only boolean value that specifies whether the window has been closed.

defaultStatus
> A read/write string that specifies a persistent message to appear in the status line whenever the browser is not displaying another message.

document
> A read-only reference to the Document object contained in this window or frame. See Document.

frames[]
> An array of Window objects, one for each frame contained within the this window. Note that frames referenced by the frames[] array may themselves contain frames and may have a frames[] array of their own.

history
> A read-only reference to the History object of this window or frame. See History.

length
> Specifies the number of frames contained in this window or frame. Same as frames.length.

location

> The Location object for this window or frame. See Location. This property has special behavior: if you assign a URL string to it, the browser loads and displays that URL.

name

> A string that contains the name of the window or frame. The name is specified with the Window.open() method, or with the name attribute of a <frame> tag. Read-only in JS 1.0; read/write in JS 1.1.

navigator

> A read-only reference to the Navigator object, which provides version and configuration information about the web browser. See Navigator.

opener

> A read/write reference to the Window that opened this window. JS 1.1.

parent

> A read-only reference to the Window object that contains this window or frame. If this window is a top-level window, parent refers to the window itself.

screen

> A read-only reference to the Screen object that specifies information about the screen the browser is running on. See Screen. JS 1.2.

self

> A read-only reference to this window itself. This is a synonym for the window property.

status

> A read/write string that can be set to display a transient message in the browser's status line.

top

> A read-only reference to the the top-level window that contains this window. If this window is a top-level window, top refers to the window itself.

window

> The window property is identical to the self property; it contains a reference to this window.

Netscape 4 Properties

`innerHeight`, `innerWidth`

Read/write properties that specify the height and width, in pixels, of the document display area of this window. These dimensions do not include the height of the menubar, toolbars, scrollbars, and so on.

`outerHeight`, `outerWidth`

Read/write integers that specify the total height and width, in pixels, of the window. These dimensions include the height and width of the menubar, toolbars, scrollbars, window borders, and so on.

`pageXOffset`, `pageYOffset`

Read-only integers that specify the number of pixels that the current document has been scrolled to the right (`pageXOffset`) and down (`pageYOffset`).

`screenX`, `screenY`

Read-only integers that specify the X and Y-coordinates of the upper-left corner of the window on the screen. If this window is a frame, these properties specify the X and Y-coordinates of the top-level window that contains the frame.

IE 4 Properties

`clientInformation`

An IE-specific synonym for the `navigator` property. Refers to the Navigator object.

`event`

The event property refers to an Event object that contains the details of the most recent event to occur within this window. In the IE event model, the Event object is not passed as an argument to the event handler, and is instead assigned to this property.

Methods

The Window object has the following portable methods. Since the Window object is the Global object in client-side JavaScript, it also defines the methods listed on the Global reference page.

alert(*message*)

Displays *message* in a dialog box. Returns nothing. JS 1.0.

blur()

Yields the keyboard focus and returns nothing. JS 1.1.

clearInterval(*intervalId*)

Cancels the periodic execution of code specified by *intervalId*. See setInterval( ). Returns nothing. JS 1.2.

clearTimeout(*timeoutId*)

Cancels the pending timeout specified by *timeoutId*. See setTimeout( ). Returns nothing. JS 1.0.

close()

Closes a window and returns nothing. JS 1.0.

confirm(*question*)

Displays *question* in a dialog box and waits for a yes-or-no response. Returns true if the user clicks the **OK** button, or false if the user clicks the **Cancel** button. JS 1.0.

focus()

Requests keyboard focus; this also brings the window to the front on most platforms. Returns nothing. JS 1.1.

getComputedStyle(*elt*)

Returns a read-only Style object that contains all CSS styles (not just inline styles) that apply to the specified document element *elt*. Positioning attributes such as left, top, and width queried from this computed style object are always returned as pixel values. DOM Level 2.

moveBy(*dx, dy*)

Moves the window the specified distances from its current position and returns nothing. JS 1.2.

moveTo(*x, y*)

Moves the window to the specified position and returns nothing. JS 1.2

open(*url, name, features*)

Displays the specified *url* in the named window. If the *name* argument is omitted or if there is no window by that name, a new window is created. The optional *features* argument is a string that specifies the size and decorations of the new window as a comma-separated list of features. Feature names commonly supported on all platforms are: width=*pixels*, height=*pixels*, location, menubar, resizable, status, and toolbar. In IE, set the position of the window with left=*x* and top=*y*. In Netscape, use screenX=*x* and screenY=*y*. Returns the existing or new Window object. JS 1.0.

print()

Simulates a click on the browser's **Print** button and returns nothing. Netscape 4; IE 5.

prompt(*message*, *default*)

Displays *message* in a dialog box and waits for the user to enter a text response. Displays the optional *default* as the default response. Returns the string entered by the user, or the empty string if the user did not enter a string, or null if the user clicked **Cancel**. JS 1.0.

resizeBy(*dw*, *dh*)

Resizes the window by the specified amount and returns nothing. JS 1.2.

resizeTo(*width*, *height*)

Resizes the window to the specified size and returns nothing. JS 1.2.

scroll(*x*, *y*)

Scrolls the window to the specified coordinates and returns nothing. JS 1.1; deprecated in JS 1.2 in favor of scrollTo( ).

scrollBy(*dx*, *dy*)

Scrolls the window by a specified amount and returns nothing. JS 1.2.

scrollTo(*x*, *y*)

Scrolls the window to a specified position and returns nothing. JS 1.2.

setInterval(*code*, *interval*, *args...*)

Evaluates the string of JavaScript *code* every *interval* milliseconds. In Netscape 4 and IE 5, *code* may be a reference to a function instead of a string. In that case, the function is invoked every *interval* milliseconds. In Netscape, any arguments after *interval* are passed to the function when it is invoked, but this feature is not supported by IE. Returns an interval ID value that can be passed to clearInterval() to cancel the periodic executions. JS 1.2.

setTimeout(*code, delay*)

Evaluates the JavaScript code in the string *code* after *delay* milliseconds have elapsed. In Netscape 4 and IE5, *code* may be a function rather than a string; see the discussion under setInterval(). Returns a timeout ID value that can be passed to clearTimeout() to cancel the pending execution of *code*. Note that this method returns immediately; it does not wait for *delay* milliseconds before returning. JS 1.0.

Event Handlers

Event handlers for a Window object are defined by attributes of the <body> tag of the document.

onblur

Invoked when the window loses focus.

onerror

Invoked when a JavaScript error occurs. This is a special event handler that is invoked with three arguments that specify the error message, the URL of the document that contained the error, and the line number of the error, if available.

onfocus

Invoked when the window gains focus.

onload

Invoked when the document (or frameset) is fully loaded.

onresize

Invoked when the window is resized.

onunload

Invoked when the browser leaves the current document.

See Also

Document

Related Titles Available from O'Reilly

Web Programming

ActionScript Cookbook

ActionScript for Flash MX
Pocket Reference

ActionScript for Flash MX:
The Definitive Guide,
2nd Edition

Creating Applications
with Mozilla

Dynamic HTML: The Definitive Reference, *2nd Edition*

Flash Remoting:
The Definitive Guide

Google Hacks

Google Pocket Guide

HTTP: The Definitive Guide

JavaScript & DHTML Cookbook

JavaScript: The Definitive Guide,
4th Edition

PHP 5 Essentials

PHP Cookbook

PHP Pocket Reference,
2nd Edition

Programming ColdFusion MX,
2nd Edition

Programming PHP

Web Database Applications
with PHP and MySQL,
2nd Edition

Webmaster in a Nutshell,
3rd Edition

Cascading Style Sheets:
The Definitive Guide,
2nd Edition

CSS Pocket Reference

Dreamweaver MX 2004:
The Missing Manual

HTML & XHTML:
The Definitive Guide,
5th Edition

HTML Pocket Reference,
2nd Edition

Information Architecture
for the World Wide Web,
2nd Edition

Learning Web Design,
2nd Edition

Web Design in a Nutshell,
2nd Edition

Web Administration

Apache Cookbook

Apache Pocket Reference

Apache: The Definitive Guide,
3rd Edition

Essential Blogging

Perl for Web Site Management

Squid: The Definitive Guide

Web Performance Tuning,
2nd Edition

Web Authoring and Design

O'REILLY®

Keep in touch with O'Reilly

1. Download examples from our books

To find example files for a book, go to:
www.oreilly.com/catalog
select the book, and follow the "Examples" link.

2. Register your O'Reilly books

Register your book at *register.oreilly.com*

Why register your books? Once you've registered your O'Reilly books you can:

- Win O'Reilly books, T-shirts or discount coupons in our monthly drawing.
- Get special offers available only to registered O'Reilly customers.
- Get catalogs announcing new books (US and UK only).
- Get email notification of new editions of the O'Reilly books you own.

3. Join our email lists

Sign up to get topic-specific email announcements of new books and conferences, special offers, and O'Reilly Network technology newsletters at:
elists.oreilly.com

It's easy to customize your free elists subscription so you'll get exactly the O'Reilly news you want.

4. Get the latest news, tips, and tools

www.oreilly.com

- "Top 100 Sites on the Web"—PC Magazine
- CIO Magazine's Web Business 50 Awards

Our web site contains a library of comprehensive product information (including book excerpts and tables of contents), downloadable software, background articles, interviews with technology leaders, links to relevant sites, book cover art, and more.

5. Work for O'Reilly

Check out our web site for current employment opportunities:
jobs.oreilly.com

6. Contact us

O'Reilly & Associates
1005 Gravenstein Hwy North
Sebastopol, CA 95472 USA

TEL: 707-827-7000 or 800-998-9938
(6am to 5pm PST)

FAX: 707-829-0104

order@oreilly.com
For answers to problems regarding your order or our products.
To place a book order online, visit:
www.oreilly.com/order_new

catalog@oreilly.com
To request a copy of our latest catalog.

booktech@oreilly.com
For book content technical questions or corrections.

corporate@oreilly.com
For educational, library, government, and corporate sales.

proposals@oreilly.com
To submit new book proposals to our editors and product managers.

international@oreilly.com
For information about our international distributors or translation queries. For a list of our distributors outside of North America check out:
international.oreilly.com/distributors.html

adoption@oreilly.com
For information about academic use of O'Reilly books, visit:
academic.oreilly.com

O'REILLY®

Our books are available at most retail and online bookstores.
To order direct: 1-800-998-9938 • *order@oreilly.com* • *www.oreilly.com*
Online editions of most O'Reilly titles are available at *safari.oreilly.com*